Mountains to Move

Charles D. Taylor

© 2015

Published in the United States by Nurturing Faith Inc., Macon GA,

www.nurturingfaith.net.

Library of Congress Cataloging-in-Publication Data is available.

ISBN 978-1-938514-78-4

All rights reserved. Printed in the United States of America

Scripture quotations are from New Revised Standard Version Bible, copyright © 1989 National Council of the Churches of Christ in the United States of America. Used by permission. All rights reserved.

Cover Photo: Anne Swoboda, flickr.com/photos/anneh632/
Creative Commons Attribution-ShareAlike 2.0 Generic

Preface

This work is a sequel to another book about the life and teachings of Jesus. It is a continuation of the story of the early church and the many obstacles it confronted. On one occasion during his ministry, Jesus told the apostles that if they had faith as great as a mustard seed, they could say to a mountain, "Get up and be cast into the sea," and it would be done. In the light of all the beautiful figures of speech that Jesus used, this one seems to follow that course. There would be no great value in moving a mountain into the sea or anywhere else, so what could he have meant? The contention of this work is that he was talking about the great hindrances, the almost impossible barriers that would confront the apostles and others in the early church. Some of them were external, and some had to do with internal attitudes. In fact, the very size of the daunting task would make many feel that it was futile to even start. If the figures are anywhere close to accurate, about 120 individuals were being asked to go out and conquer the world. That looked impossible, not only because of the fantastic odds they faced, but because of the many racial, cultural, and religious obstacles that they were to face. Instead of talking about literal mountains, Jesus was probably indicating that, with faith, they could accomplish tasks that appeared to be overwhelming. They confronted much opposition, but with faith and the empowering of the Holy Spirit, they did move mountains.

This work will use the New Revised Standard Version of the New Testament as the base material. There are several reasons for this choice. First, the text is translated from the best Greek texts available, using recent manuscript discoveries. The use of textual criticism is an ongoing effort, and therefore offers the best texts available. Second, living languages are constantly changing. The King James Version may present some beautiful old English, but the message may be blurred because of language changes. Once, just after the Revised Standard Version came out and numerous arguments were being offered against it, I was talking with a man about the need for new translations. He told me, "If the King James was good enough for Paul, it is good enough for me." Needless to say, the discussion ended at that point. When that type of ignorance prevails, there is little possibility of learning. Ignorance simply means a lack of knowledge and understanding, and every person is ignorant in areas where expertise is lacking. It is not the same as mental inability or stupidity. So the claim for constant diligence in making better translations should be obvious. As an example, in I Thessalonians 4:15, where Paul discusses the concept of resurrection of the dead and the return of the Lord, the KJV translates the verse as, "We which are alive and remain unto the coming of the Lord shall not prevent them which are asleep." In the modern era, "prevent" has lost its former meaning and now means "to stop" or "hinder." But any student probably knows that in 1611 C.E., the term "prevent" meant "to go before." So from the KJV the verse seems to indicate that, in some sense, Paul was saying that in no way could those who are alive hinder those who have already died, as if literally (and that was the thought in those days) it meant that those who are alive could stand on the graves or bar the doors of a tomb and keep the resurrection of those who have died from happening. That was not Paul's message, but language barriers can distort the message.

This work, then, is an effort to show some of the problems the early church faced and to demonstrate how those issues were solved. It will use as a framework the book of Acts, and when issues arise such as those that brought about the book of Galatians and the Corinthian correspondence, it will include them. The scripture texts will be indicated but will not be printed. This is a running narrative of what appears to have been happening in the early church. Often, one hears someone say that they would like to have lived in the early days of the church, when there were no problems. That kind of statement betrays a lack of knowledge about the struggles, both internal and external, that beset the early church. What follows is a result of a class taught in two different universities and to numerous church groups. There will always be a great debt owed to my college and seminary professors and to many insightful students who contributed to this study through many penetrating questions.

It will become evident that, to this writer, the kind of exclusiveness and the legalistic position that developed from the time of Ezra became a huge impediment. While one can sympathize with Ezra and perhaps sense how legalism developed, the experience of Abraham, Isaac, Jacob, and Joseph had been that of faith and following in obedience. Most likely such a rigid legalistic system was never God's intention, for all genuine devotees had followed in faith. In one sense, "legalism" hijacked fundamental Judaism and, therefore, presented a major mountain for the pioneer followers.

Contents

Preface v

Chapter 1: An Introduction to the Book of Acts 1
Chapter 2: The Community Moves On 5
Chapter 3: The Promised Power 9
Chapter 4: Ugly Conflicts Arise 12
Chapter 5: Disruption in the Community 15
Chapter 6: A Door Opens to the World 21
Chapter 7: A New Instrument for the Living Lord 27
Chapter 8: A Giant Step Forward 33
Chapter 9: The Center Shifts 39
Chapter 10: An Incredible Advance 46
Chapter 11: The Basic Question: Is Salvation by Grace? 54
Chapter 12: Further Expansion to the Gentiles 60
Chapter 13: The Controversy Carried to Galatia 63
Chapter 14: Retrogression Denies Abraham's Experience 69
Chapter 15: An Appeal for Personal Loyalty 75
Chapter 16: Freedom and Moral Responsibility 80
Chapter 17: A New Vision 84
Chapter 18: The Ministry in Ephesus 97
Chapter 19: The Nature of the Corinthian Correspondence 101
Chapter 20: Some of the Problems at Corinth 104
Chapter 21: Matters Necessitating Discipline 108
Chapter 22: Specific Questions from Corinth 112

Chapter 23: Idolatry and Related Problems 116
Chapter 24: The Journey Comes to Its Conclusion 130
Chapter 25: The Return to Jerusalem 135
Chapter 26: Paul Removed from Jerusalem 144
Chapter 27: Destination Rome..149

Bibliography..156

Chapter 1

An Introduction to the Book of Acts

One of the most valuable recent contributions to the study of the book of Acts has been that of Frank Stagg. He has pointed out (as R.R. Williams had done earlier in the Acts volume of the Torch Bible Commentaries) that the book shows how, regardless of difficulties and dangers, the gospel overcame all hurdles and moved on "unhindered."

"An adverb is a strange word to end a book, but Luke did just that. In fact, the two volume work, Luke-Acts, is brought to a dramatic close and epitomized in an adverb. (The Greek word *akolutos* is an adverb translated literally as "unhinderedly.") Throughout his two volumes Luke never lost sight of his purpose, he planned well the conclusion of it, achieving the final effort by the last stroke of the pen.

"Unhinderedly," Luke wrote, describing the hard–won liberty of the gospel. This liberty came only after many barriers had been crossed, and it won because its first home was in the mind and intention of Jesus himself."[1]

Purpose

The ending of the book of Acts is somewhat puzzling. One cannot help but wonder if the book is incomplete, because at first sight the ending seems abrupt. It leads to the question about whether the book concludes with all that Luke knew at the time of writing. Of course, if that is the case, the date for Acts must be pushed back far earlier than the time to which most scholars assign it, for the last information leaves us at about 64/65 C.E., with Paul living in "his own hired dwelling." But that date is not consistent with the concept that Luke's gospel, which must be the "former treatise" referred to in Acts 1, was written somewhere around 75 C.E. at the earliest. Therefore, one must conclude that the purpose of the book had been achieved with those ending words.

The author's purpose for this work is not to show geographical expansion or to follow the deeds of the apostles, but to demonstrate the progress of the movement from its inception as a small Jewish sect until it overcame all barriers (removed mountains) and became a religion for all the world. The book of Acts is more than history, although it contains much historical material. It appears to demonstrate how the gospel progressed according to "the Spirit of Jesus," and it created a record of the efforts of the church to maintain the unity of the body of Christ.

The New Testament term "church" is used in two ways. Its primary meaning is that of an organism, a living body. That meaning underlies every usage of the term. If one relies solely on the number of times the word appears to refer to a local institution, there are more uses referring to the institution than to an organism. That is because of the letters written to local churches, but it does not in any way lessen the fundamental meaning of the term *ekklesia*. One of the barriers that Luke may have seen was that Christianity needed to be seen as a *religion licita*. The Roman government appears to have lumped religions into one of two categories: *religio illicita*, which would have included unrecognized religions (and while they were not illegal, they would have been circumscribed by certain limitations), or *religio licita*, which would have referred to a recognized religion with certain protections. Incidentally, one of the values inherited by the movement from its Jewish parent was that Judaism was a *religio licita*, and for some time the new movement was seen as another sect of Judaism.

That could have been one of the sub-motives. It could have been needed because at the conclusion of the Jewish War (70 C.E.) it was suddenly evident that Christianity and Judaism were not the same. But the primary purpose of the book of Acts seems to have been to demonstrate how the gospel message overcame religious, racial, cultural, and national barriers. It was easier, even during the first century, to overcome geographical barriers than other major obstacles.

Authorship

The book of Acts is the source of most of our information about the spread of Christianity until it reached universal proportions. The story began around 30 C.E. at the death and resurrection of Jesus and continued until 64/65 C.E. The name of the book, as seen in the manuscript "Sinaiticus," was simply *Praxis*, which means "works" or "deeds." The book is found in one of the earliest listings

An Introduction to the Book of Acts

of accepted works called the Muratorian Canon @175-200 C.E. The prologue of the book links it with the authorship of the gospel of Luke.

> Since many have undertaken to set down an orderly account of the events that have been fulfilled among us, 2 just as they were handed on to us by those who from the beginning were eyewitnesses and servants of the word, 3 I, too, decided after investigating everything from the first, to write an orderly account for you, most excellent Theophilus, 4 So that you may know the truth concerning the things about which we have been instructed. (Luke 1:1-4)

> In the first book, Theophilus, I wrote about all that Jesus did and taught from the beginning, 2 until the day when he was taken up to heaven after giving instruction through the Holy Spirit to the apostles whom he had chosen. (Acts 1:1-2)

Two things are obvious: (a) This author was not an eyewitness to the gospel events, but he was a careful editor of what he wrote. (b) Not only do these two works share the same recipient, but the information dovetails so carefully that they almost form one unit, which suggests that they were either written by the same person or that one of them is expertly pseudonymous.

Often in the ancient world, things were written by one author in the spirit of a previous worthy and credited under the name of the ancient person. But in this case, there is little reason to doubt that these works were written by the same person. That the author was Luke is reinforced in the book of Acts, beginning in Chapter 16, verse 11, when the writer suddenly begins to use the first person, saying, "We did this" and "we" went here or there. By examining the epistles of Colossians, Ephesians, Philippians, and Philemon, it is easy to see that Luke was present when the first personal pronoun was used in the book of Acts. There were only two people we know of who seem to have always been present with Paul at those times. They were, Jesus Justus, a Jew and a relatively unknown/obscure person, and Luke, who was a Gentile and who "fits" everything. When Luke was not present, Acts reverts to the third person pronoun "they." There is scant evidence "pro" or "con" that Luke was a Macedonian, but the initial usage of that first person pronoun occurred immediately after Paul had the vision asking him to come to Macedonia. Could Luke be the subconscious source for that vision/dream?

One also needs to be aware that the Koine' Greek used in both Luke and Acts is similar and is very good Greek. Numerous scholars have noted that the best Greek in the New Testament is in these two books and in the book of Hebrews. Therefore, the conclusion that the author of these two works was a native of Greece and that the two works are inextricably intertwined is almost irrefutable.[2]

Luke was an educated Greek; in Colossians, he was called "the beloved physician." In both the gospel and in Acts, there is evidence of an affectionate, caring nature and a concern about the danger of riches, the problems of greed as seen in the lives of Ananias and Sapphira, the unfair handling of money in regard to the Hellenistic widows, and the beautiful value of the *koinonia*. That same interest is seen in the Lucan version of the beatitude, "Blessed are the poor." There is also considerable interest and concern about the effects of divisiveness, which would be characteristic of what we know about Luke.

Date

Accepting these conclusions, certain limits are placed in terms of the date of writing. Obviously, it could not have been written before the last information in the work. Therefore, the earliest possible date would be 64/65 C.E., and the latest would be the death of Luke. We have no information about his death, but a good conjecture would be around 95/100 C.E. These limits can be narrowed because Acts was probably written soon after the gospel (see the prologues of the two books), and nearly all scholars place the date for the writing of Luke's gospel around 75/80 C.E. This would most likely place the date for the composition of Acts around 85 C.E.

[1]Frank Stagg, *The Book of Acts* (Nashville: The Broadman Press, 1955), 1.
[2]Richard Belward Rackham, *The Acts of the Apostles* (London: Metheuen and Co. Ltd., 1951), xvi-xvii.

Chapter 2

The Community Moves On

Anyone who has studied the record of the resurrection appearances of Jesus will immediately recognize the difficulty in putting them in order. There were appearances in both Galilee and Jerusalem, and the various gospels give differing accounts, both to number and location. Then there is a statement by Paul that Jesus appeared to more than 500. Perhaps all that needs to be said here is that something totally out of the ordinary had occurred, and it transformed the timid group of apostles into an unbelievably courageous band. Nothing else could have removed their sense of gloom and loss of purpose.

They were told to wait in Jerusalem for some unique experience which would provide power for them. There was some difference in being in the presence of Jesus and coming to be under the Holy Spirit. Jesus seems to have indicated that just as John's baptism offered to his followers a new challenge, this new baptism in the spirit would provide energy and power for the new life. But the apostles were still confused. The old national concept of the kingdom of Israel, which had bothered them throughout the ministry of Jesus, was still with them, and they asked if it were now to become a reality (1:6). This probably represents the very first mountain that the early church had to remove, and it was a major one, since it was likely based on the old Mosaic interpretation of the nation and the covenant made with Father Abraham. (Genesis 12:1-3) Some parts of the covenant were not emphasized during the period between the last prophetic voice and the time of Jesus, but under the rule of numerous foreign powers there was a chafing and a hope that Israel would be restored to its Davidic and Solomonic glory and power. That hope had seen the willingness of many to follow anyone who made the claim of Messiah-ship, most of them in a military way. Since Jesus had so often used parables to illustrate the concept of the kingdom (but in the canonical materials he never defined it), it is not surprising that they had not understood. Probably the only issue for many first-century Jews was: *when will God bring this about?* Note that in the listing of the disciples in verse 13, Simon the Zealot is still among them, so there was at least one who held to that national obsession, and probably all of the disciples were infected. (Recall the desire of James and John, or their mother, that the two of them should be the right and left hand men in the kingdom.) One cannot help but wonder if the failure to get the spiritual and universal part of the message across was not due to their preconceptions. It may be observed that even in the twenty-first century there are still those who believe the kingdom has been or will be restored to the nation. Although the Zionist movement is the strong center of such thought, there are also Christians who believe it.

Jesus' answer is intriguing. He seems to say, "That is none of your business – it belongs to God only, but your task is to be witnesses." Therefore, he related their responsibility to witnessing to *the entire world* about the kingdom. That challenge sounds much like the Great Commission in Matthew 28:19-20.

It is interesting that in this challenge he moved from Jerusalem to Samaria and finally to the whole world. Remember that this commits them to crossing all barriers — geographical, religious, racial, and cultural. The record in the book of Acts shows how challenging it was. So now, the immediate quasi-physical appearance of Jesus was leaving; he was moving completely from the material to the spiritual realm. In a time when the entire inhabited world placed the cosmological understanding of hell as an underground region and the heavenly realm in the skies, how else could they have expressed what happened in any other way than to say, "He was taken up?" The text may mean that a cloud obscured him, but the "how" of the ascension is still beyond explanation. (Even the word "ascension" to describe Jesus' leaving reflects that same cosmology.) A number of questions must have flooded their minds. What did it mean that he would return? How soon would this take place? What is to be done in the meantime? The forty-day period had been a time of assurance that all was not lost, but the only direction that they had was to wait.

Acts 1:12-26

The small group of intimate followers gathered, probably in the same "upper room" that they had used previously. Bewildered or not, the little community gathered for prayer. As Luke recorded it, the group included the eleven and some women; he specifically mentioned Mary, the mother of Jesus, and for the first time the brothers of Jesus were included. (As most believers know, there is some disagreement about who those brothers and sisters were. Most Protestant followers simply consider them to have been the children of Joseph and Mary who were born after Jesus. However, especially since the desire arose to protect the perpetual virginity of Mary and since the idea arose that abstention from sexual activity was somehow on a higher moral plane than involvement in the normal sexual relationships of marriage, some conclude that these children were either Joseph's from a former marriage or they were cousins. For our purposes in this study, the issue is irrelevant.)

The death of Judas is referred to only in this passage and in the gospel of Matthew (from the "M" source?) There are variations in the accounts. In the Matthew account, Judas is said to have hanged himself with no mention of any other dramatic end, as Acts suggests. The Matthew account tells of Judas throwing down the coins in the presence of the members of the Sanhedrin, which shows some sort of awareness on his part that he had been horribly in error, and that they, attempting to not contaminate the temple treasury, took the money and bought a field. Acts states that Judas bought the field. There is also a difference in that Matthew simply states that Judas hanged himself, while the Acts account suggests a more gruesome end in that Judas "burst open and all of his bowels gushed out." There have been those who have tried to explain the difference by indicating that Judas did indeed hang himself and that his body was exposed for a long enough time that it became swollen. When it was cut down, it fell and burst. For many, there may be no need to reconcile the accounts. They may simply be two accounts that existed in the oral transmission, and since there was no real conflict in the essence of the story, trying to make them agree was unnecessary.

Literary practices vary from the first century to the twenty-first, and current literary practices simply do not apply. We have little information about what restrictions, if any, first-century writers observed. We do know that they often seemed to be at liberty to fill out or compose speeches. Only the gist may have been preserved, and certain common stories or ideas may have been used to represent an idea of something like the death of a traitor.

In that regard, the following story is of interest:

Ahiqar was a trusted advisor of King Sennacherib. He had no children, so he adopted the son of his daughter, Nathan (or Nadan), brought him up, and educated him as his own offspring. But the youth turned out ill and betrayed his father by forging documents of treasonable nature. As a result, Ahiqar was condemned to be executed. A plan was devised by Ahiqar's wife and friends, and a condemned criminal, Senigar (whose appearance was very much like that of Ahiqar), was dressed in Ahiqar's clothes and executed. Ahiqar was then hidden in his cellar to await the outcome of the events. Later, Sennacherib was unable to meet the intrigues of Pharaoh of Egypt and stated that if Ahiqar were alive, he would give the needed advice. Much to the king's amazement, he is told that Ahiqar is alive. Ahiqar emerges from his hiding place with long, matted hair and nails almost like claws, and is restored to his former place of trust. He, in turn, imprisons the traitorous son and starves him to death.

> "And when Nadan heard that speech from his uncle, Haiqara, he swelled up immediately and became like a blown out bladder. And his limbs swelled, his hands and feet and his side, and he was torn and his belly burst asunder and his entrails were scattered, he perished and died." (Arabic version)

> "In the same hour Nathan swelled up and his body burst asunder." (Armenian version)

Both accounts tell of the death of a traitor. But the Armenian closely resembles the Acts 1:18 narrative.[1]

In looking at this summary, at least three things are possible. First, the story of Nathan's death may have become a common story which illustrated the death of a traitor, much like the assassination of Caesar became a symbol for treachery (*et tu Brute*), or the concept of Achilles' heel became a symbol for one's weakest spot. Luke may have known the story and used it to demonstrate the demise of the traitor of the Lord, so that the selection of Matthias could be explained. Second, someone later might have added this account to Luke's account to explain why the selection of Matthias was necessary. Third, there may be no connection at all between Luke's writing and the Ahiqar story, and some other explanation of the differences between the accounts could be given.

Whatever one thinks of all of that, the number of apostles had been reduced to eleven. There was an understanding that the number needed to be completed as witnesses of the resurrection, but the twelfth needed to have shared in the total ministry of Jesus, including the resurrection. Apparently one reason for adding to the group was because Judas had forfeited his position. (Luke used a proof text from Psalm 109:8.) Twelve was the number Jesus had chosen, and it corresponded to the twelve tribes of Israel.

Two men, Joseph Barsabbas (also known as Justus) and Matthias, were chosen and then selected by lots. Perhaps that was some form of voting, and Matthias won. Beyond this, we know little about these men. Apparently, this re-filling did not become a tradition, for there is no indication that the number was replenished when James, the brother of John, was killed.

---

[1] R.H. Charles, *The Apocrypha and Pseudepigrapha* (London: Oxford Press, 1913), 715-776.

Chapter 3

The Promised Power

Waiting is hard because it is filled with uncertainty, as the disciples discovered. Even though Jesus had instructed them and those with them to wait, they did not know what to expect.

Acts 2:1-13

What an amazing day! It is extremely difficult to know exactly what did happen, except that an extraordinary event occurred. The symbols of wind and fire used to describe the experience of the power of God coming on each of the followers should be seen as an attempt to show the significance of that day. The unusual sound could only be described as something like a violent wind blowing. Every one of the believers was gloriously touched by this outpouring. That does not mean that some outside believer would have seen literal fire touching them, but rather it is a figure to show that every believer received a blessing. (After all, Luke did write "like a wind" and "as of fire.")

Neither is it certain how the miracle of understanding took place. There are statements in the narrative that make one believe that, for this unique event, the little company was speaking in languages other than Aramaic. But there are other indications that the miracle was that people could understand in their own native language. Those who are listed as being present are Jews or proselytes from various parts of the empire. The general consensus has been that all of the disciples were enabled to speak in languages other than their own. And yet, there were those who heard but did not understand, who disparaged the event by indicating that those speaking were drunk, lending support to the theory that the miracle was in the hearing.

Some interpreters have suggested that the Holy Spirit came for the first time on that day. This idea does not seem to be sustainable, since there are recorded appearances of the Holy Spirit in the Old Testament. Jesus even breathed on the disciples and said, "Receive the Spirit." In fact, in Peter's first speech in Acts 1, he indicated that the Holy Spirit had spoken through David. Still others have suggested that prior to this day the Holy Spirit came on people externally, but at this time it became an indwelling force. This distinction is also difficult to maintain because there is no reason, other than to enforce the uniqueness of this event, to believe that the Spirit of God just took over people, regardless of their wills. He always seems to have worked with them and through them in the same way he worked with the people of the first-century church, never violating the free will of any human. What then was this event?

Keep in mind that the presence of Jesus, as they had known him, was gone. They must have felt in some sense that they were alone again, so they needed some assurance that they were not orphans. Now they indeed felt that they had received the promised continuing presence and guidance of the Holy Spirit. In the long discourse in John 14-17, written long after this event, Jesus promised that he would not leave the disciples alone, but he would be with them in the Spirit. That immediately forces one to try to think about the nature of the Godhead, and no discussion of that has ever been satisfactory. As everyone knows, Christianity has been accused by some as teaching that there are three gods. This may be because the teaching of the church regarding what is called the Trinity is so confusing. It would seem that, even with the difficulties of the limitations placed on the divine nature of Jesus during his earthly sojourn, there is one God experienced in several ways. Part of the difficulty is because humans have no way to think of or explain what we call the "spirit realm" except through symbols. But when one thinks of God as the Eternal Creator and Sustainer of the universe, it is necessary to see him as Father, because that is what Jesus called him. (In dealing with God, it has been customary to speak in masculine terms.) When one speaks of God in relation to his redeeming nature and activity, one uses the figure of the redemptive son, the earthly Jesus. (It would be fair to say that the son-ship idea is not a physically procreative issue, but a figure to express the unity of God. In fact, there are places where the term *pais*, meaning servant, is used, and that avoids the normal implications of the term "son.") When one speaks of God as the teaching and directing spiritual force, the concept of the Holy Spirit is used. So while the creeds speak (in a rather confusing fashion) of three "persons," there cannot be three separate individuals. In fact, St. Paul said to the people of Corinth in II Corinthians 3:17-18, "Now the Lord is the Spirit, and where the Spirit of the Lord is, there is freedom. And all of us, with unveiled faces, seeing the glory of the Lord as though reflected in a mirror, are being transformed into the same image from one degree of glory to another, for this comes from the Lord, who is the Spirit." This is a simple and straightforward statement, *"ho de kurios to pneuma estin."* The last phrase in the paragraph is one of apposition, *"apo kuriou pneumatos."* Each of the terms is in the genitive case and must be in apposition, so it means simply, "the Lord who is the Spirit."

Chapter 4

Ugly Conflicts Arise

❖

The little movement was still a part of the larger Jewish religious community, and there was probably no idea, as yet, of separation — until it was forced on the group. Publicity has a way of bringing out conflicts.

Acts 3:1-26

Peter and John were still good Jews and they were going, as was their custom, into the temple for the hour of prayer. There were no government programs to sustain an invalid man, and he sat at the temple gate to beg for alms. To his astonishment, instead of money, his infirmity was healed. This was the first recorded miracle performed in the early community, and it demonstrated to all that there was real power in the new movement. Peter used this event as an opportunity to explain the purpose of Jesus in the work of God. (Jesus is identified as having been linked tightly with the purposes of God throughout the Old Testament record, beginning with Abraham.) Peter again did not exonerate the people, but he specifically held the Jewish religious leaders responsible for the death of Jesus.

There is an interesting concept here (verse 13) which had not been expressed before that Pilate had decided to release him. We have no information in the gospels regarding this except that Pilate found no cause for the death penalty. That issue may have been in some of Peter's oral statements, but it must have never reached the level of being an official part of Peter's contribution, for Mark did not include it. It would appear that they saw that the purpose of Jesus' life was to offer new life to the people, if they would repent. Notice how closely this message follows the *kerygma*. The healing is attributed to the power of God, but also to the power and the name of Jesus. This perhaps brings us to the first time the servant concept was linked this closely to God's purposes.

Acts 4:1-4

While it is fairly certain that the movement would never have continued had it not been for the resurrection, it is the concept of "resurrection" itself that caused the ensuing problem. This mountain is really an external one. Jesus had experienced the same "run-in" with the Sadducees, who were vehemently opposed to any idea of resurrection. But even though he had quieted them and argumentatively defeated them, they had not changed their minds. The one element in the preaching of Peter and John that these religious leaders used to confront them was the resurrection concept. There certainly must have been some anger because they had been accused of being responsible for the death of Jesus, but this was the first time that they, relying on their own teaching, made the challenge regarding the resurrection. Any careful study of the religious issues confronting the Jewish people will find that the doctrine developed late in their history, and some segments of modern Judaism still do not accept an after-life. It was by the power of the temple, its priests, and the captain of its police that Peter and John were taken out of circulation. The central doctrine or teaching of the early church, the one its very life depended on, was the resurrection of Jesus, and that was the issue that brought them before the Sanhedrin. The message moved on in an unhindered fashion as the number increased to 5,000. But what was to happen to the church leaders?

Acts 4:5-31

This first confrontation with the Jewish leaders since the death of Jesus was held at a formal meeting of the Sanhedrin. It has often been noted that Annas was not the high priest at this time. He had been deposed by the Romans because of corruption. Caiaphas, his son-in-law who was the current high priest, was also present. That, however, did not stop the influence of Annas with the Sanhedrin, which may have been the reason Luke called him high priest. (One element that may have influenced the attitude of Annas was that he seems to have been in charge of the booths in the temple where sacrificial animals were sold and where money was changed into shekels for payment of the temple tax. Jesus had directly attacked his authority when he "cleansed" the Temple.) The Sanhedrin was responsible for handling religious disputes, and at this formal meeting the accused were required to stand in the center of the group and reply to the charges. It was probably to get the charges stated plainly and for the record that they asked Peter and John by what authority they had done this sign. One cannot help but surmise that they already knew the answer, but Peter, who just a few weeks before had been afraid to admit that he even knew Jesus, now stated with glaring boldness that the power behind this event was Jesus. He further affirmed that the Sanhedrin was responsible for the death of Jesus and that, in spite of their efforts, God had raised him from the dead. It was also Peter's contention that there was no other in whom they could find salvation. Since he was speaking to a Jewish court about a Messiah, his statement may mean that this one (Jesus) is God's promised deliverer and that there will be no other. In current times, this passage has been used to support the exclusivist argument. Whether that was Peter's intention or not is open for debate.

Peter's declaration caused the Sanhedrin to go into closed session to decide what they must do. We can surmise that Luke was able to get the information from someone like Joseph of Arimathea, who was a member of the Sanhedrin, or perhaps even from Paul. Peter and John were not "ignorant and unlearned" men, as the King James Version translated the phrase. What the Sanhedrin saw was two men who had no rabbinical position, no formal religious training (or as it might be said in our time, no seminary degree). They were just common men, not appointed leaders, and yet they were able to expound with great fervor a theological position which came from Psalm 118:22, that "the stone which was rejected by you has become the keystone." This challenged the authority of the religious leaders. As they tried to do some damage control, their decision was that there be no further reference to the name of Jesus. There was no challenge to the healing — it could hardly be denied. But this first external mountain, an effort to stop the movement, resulted in nothing more than a warning. Peter immediately indicated that the warning would have no effect.

In one sense, this confrontation had resulted in a victory for Peter and John, but the battle was far from over. After their release, they reported the outcome to the gathered body, and there was great joy expressed because no amount of amassed human power (Herod, Pilate, the Sanhedrin, or any other) had stopped what God in Christ had set in motion. Their prayer was not for deliverance, but for boldness to confront whatever might lie ahead.

During those first days, there had been evidence of a beautiful spirit of unity. That idyllic atmosphere was soon to be violated. Already there had been some hint of the community of goods that prevailed in the group, and there is further description of that sharing in the last part of Chapter 4.

Chapter 5

Disruption in the Community

Acts 4:32-5:11

Several things are important as the story develops. First, there must have been an almost unanimous agreement to sell "stuff" and support the community. As has already been mentioned, the idea may have developed because of the belief that the Lord would return quickly and the end would come. If that were to be the case, there would be no need to own anything. Second, there was a spirit of unity that has seldom been matched in the history of the church. That experience lasted for only a short time. Later, there are people who have possessions, and no effort seems to have been made to place any communal pressure on them. Yet there must have been some honor given to those who did sell their holdings. Barnabas was one, and the narrative implies that he sold a field and brought the entire amount from the sale to the apostles. Reading between the lines, one cannot help but wonder if Barnabas was praised for that act. Jealousy and competition for praise have always plagued humanity and the church, both in the early church and in its subsequent history. It cannot be ascertained with certainty, but Ananias and Sapphira appear to have desired recognition, yet were not willing to do as Barnabas had done. So the fellowship was disrupted by their desire. It is perfectly evident from what Peter said to Ananias that he had complete freedom over his property, both to sell and to offer a portion of the proceeds to the church. That was not the problem. The issue came with the deceit that accompanied the act.

In dealing with the demise of Ananias and Sapphira, one needs to recall the tremendous awe, almost compulsive fright, that accompanied the concept of Yahweh for the Jewish people. In the early commandment, one is charged never to use the name of Yahweh in a meaningless fashion, i.e. "in vain." The modern world has lost that concept of awe and reverence so that neither the name of God nor the things dedicated to him demand that respect. In nearly all early religions, the concept of "taboo" played a vital role. It should be no surprise that there was a taboo in regard to the things of God, especially the Ark of the Covenant and the Holy of Holies. When the Ark was constructed, rings were placed in the sides so that it might be transported. No one touched it. On one occasion, when David was having the Ark moved, one man, Uzziah, reached out to keep it from falling off the cart on which it had been placed, and immediately he died. (II Samuel 6:6) In one sense, the awe of/for God kept people from him and seemed to preserve the "otherness" of God. The Hebrews were especially conscious of those things, and to involve God in a lie was a most tragic act. Therefore, when both Ananias and Sapphira were confronted with the horror of what they had done, making the Spirit a party to their lie, they died. To a modern this might seem almost unthinkable, but to a first-century Jew it would be almost inevitable.

There also is a thought in regard to the church. It has never been man's church; it always was, and still is, Christ's. Therefore, any deceitful dealing in the church is seen to be against the Holy Spirit, and as a result the evil is compounded. So while the narrative concerning the deaths of Ananias and Sapphira appears to be shocking, this disruption carried serious consequences, and the seriousness of the event emphasized the respect that should be given to the church. The inner trust and unity of the community has never been quite the same since that rupture. The narrative indicates that great fear, awe, or respect came upon all who heard of this event.

Acts 5:12-16

Signs and wonders were not uncommon in the first-century world, and they were very common at this stage of the life of the church. Peter and others were held in great awe, partly because of what happened to Ananias and Sapphira and partly because of the same healing power which they had shared when Jesus sent them forth on the mission of the seventy. (Luke 10:17-20) An interesting question remains: What did Luke mean when he wrote that "none of the rest dared to join them?" Was it that none of the people of the church dared to join the apostles or usurp their position, or was it that that those outside the group were afraid to get close? If the latter is the case, one must ask, where did the new converts come from? It was almost inevitable that superstitions would grow up around the actions of the apostles, such as some of the people wanting Peter's shadow to fall on them. These apostles held positions of respect. They confronted the same temptation that Paul and Barnabas did later when the Galatian people tried to worship them.

Acts 5:17-42

The outright disobedience of the Sanhedrin's order made it obvious to the religious leaders that something had to be done. The popularity of the apostles and what they were doing placed the authority of the Sanhedrin in jeopardy. Some of the jealousy must have had something to do with the precarious position in which the high priest found himself. At this point, Luke did not refer by name to the high priest, but whether the action was taken by Annas, who had no official authority, or by Caiaphas, it had been a rejection of the authority of the Sanhedrin's authority. The apostles — we cannot know whether this meant only Peter and John — were placed in prison. With the deliverance story, Luke clearly meant to show that the release was due to the action of God. Whether there was a human instrument or some kind of supernatural intervention, the release was a complete surprise to the Sanhedrin. They were doubly amazed to find that the prisoners were in the temple doing exactly what had they had been forbidden to do. The apostles were brought in for another hearing. The answer that Peter and the apostles gave again placed the responsibility for the death of Jesus on the religious leadership.

The term describing the response of the Sanhedrin is hard to translate into English with its full impact. It literally means "they were sawn asunder," and the translation "they were enraged" can hardly carry that force. But there is no question that the only appropriate punishment they saw was death.

The Sanhedrin was composed of both Pharisees and Sadducees, and while the initial reason for trying to put the apostles out of action was the concept of resurrection, it was not the major issue. Something had to be done to stop or counter the accusation that the leaders were responsible for the death of Jesus, and even more pressing, the deliberate affront to the Sanhedrin's authority. On the scene came a calm force. All commentators indicate that Gamaliel was a highly respected teacher, probably from the Hillel school of thought. His advice, while he did not suggest the flogging, was respected and followed.

Scholars who comment on this passage recognize that there is difficulty with the character that Gamaliel's speech referred to as Theudas. The only Theudas referred to in Josephus was involved in a fiasco about thirteen years after this speech was given. (The reference can hardly be blamed on Gamaliel, since it had not yet occurred.[1]) Either the sources Luke used were inaccurate or there was another Theudas of whom we have no record. The Theudas we know of promised a group of rebels, probably Zealots, that he would lead them to the River Jordan and then, somewhat in the fashion of Joshua, part the waters so they could cross without incident. Fadus, the Roman governor, pursued and slaughtered many of them. Theudas was captured and beheaded, and his head was taken to Jerusalem. (The reason for using this reference fits perfectly with the purpose of the Gamaliel speech.) His was a futile effort which came to nothing because it was humanly inspired. The same can be said of the revolt led by Judas. This revolt fits perfectly. In 6 B.C.E., Quirenius was governor of Syria and took a census of the area. The census was the cause of a rebellion led by Judas of Gamala, and it also came to a disastrous end.[2] The conflict may not have ended completely, for many scholars believe that the source of the Zealot sect may have been this rebellion. One must remember the literary methods and practices of the era. There were no recording tools, and often the speeches themselves were composed by the writer, using the essence of the speech as the sources gave it. If Luke's sources concerning this reference were in error, that does not in any way invalidate the argument made by Gamaliel. His purpose was to show that the movements came to naught because they were inspired by humanity. His wise advice was to let these people alone, for if what they represented was simply human, it would perish. However, with keen insight, Gamaliel added that if the movement happened to be God-inspired, the Sanhedrin could find themselves opposing God. No one can determine from this account what Gamaliel thought of this new movement, but it was a no-win situation for the Sanhedrin. His advice was that letting the movement alone would be the wisest course and, except for the flogging, the apostles escaped this persecution and overcame a mountain of opposition. The apostles paid absolutely no attention to the warning. (It may be a sneak preview, but Gamaliel was the teacher under whom Saul/Paul studied, and later we shall see that there were some "goads" against which he was struggling. Could it be that one of them was the warning that they might find themselves against God?)

The beautiful time of sharing and having all things in common brought an issue to light which was to plague the church for years. In the little church there were several groups. The core of the church had been conservatively Jewish. Jesus himself was a Jew, and so were all of the apostles. But there were others present at Pentecost, probably from the Dispersion, who were described by Luke as "Hellenists." In the atmosphere of caring for everyone, there were Hebrew and Hellenistic widows. In what may be the first culture clash, the Hellenists believed that the Hebrew widows were getting better treatment than they were. While the Hellenistic wing still had a Jewish foundation, the issue did bring to light another problem, that of racial discrimination. Evidently, the task had become so complex that it had to be taken seriously.

Disruption in the Community

Acts 6:1-6

At this point, something new or different enters the narrative. It is necessary to remember our thesis, which develops rapidly from this point on. Luke is demonstrating how the gospel moves from a small Jewish sect, overcoming impossible barriers, until it becomes a universal movement. To this point, everything has been flavored by Jewish particularism. As has been alluded to, all of the earliest followers were and continued to be good Hebrews. Except for a few occasions when smaller groups met in a "room," the worship experiences were in the temple or synagogues.

Some time must have elapsed between the introduction of the Hellenists and the account which is now considered. These Hellenists were likely Greek-speaking Jews, maybe some who lived out in the dispersion and even some from Antioch. Many scholars believe that this is a point where Luke began to use a new source. However one views it, there are now two distinct groups, the original Hebrew disciples and newer Hellenists. Those Hebrews were powerfully influenced by Jewish nationalist thoughts, but the Hellenists saw a much wider implication, to be seen in the speech of Stephen.

Human nature has not changed much over the years, and even among those who call themselves "redeemed," there are still issues. It must be said, to the credit of the early community, that they met the issue of divisiveness head-on, and that the solution proposed by the apostles was wise. Already the division of the community into "Hebrew" and "Hellenistic" wings suggests that the unity had been strained. The potential for favoritism, intentional or somewhat accidental, was inherent in the community once it began to attract new people.

It is interesting that the men who were selected for the administration of the mundane affairs all had Hellenistic names. This internal mountain of nationalism was one that the church had to conquer, or else it would divide the body of Christ. Often people see these men as the first deacons, but other than that the term *diakonos* means "one who serves" and that they "laid hands on them," it may be stretching a point to say that this new part of church organization was the beginning of the office of deacon. It will be noted later that in any situation where people were set apart for a task, the community laid hands on them. So perhaps in this special situation, this was an "ad hoc" committee to handle the issue. Another mountain had been discovered which had to be addressed and overcome if the church should later become a factor in the sense that the gospel applied to all men. An interesting side comment was that many priests were included in the community and that may reflect dissatisfaction within the priestly ranks, which ultimately produced the Covenanters of Damascus.[3]

The newly mentioned Hellenists had begun to raise some issues from a more progressive point of view. But they also may have sensed more accurately than others that the message that would soon be offered by Stephen was filled with ramifications about what this would mean for Hebrew culture and religion. However, it all begins to pry open a new door, and so the high priest asks, "Are these things so?"

[1] Flavius Josephus, *Antiquities of the Jews* (Philadelphia: Henry Coates & Co., trans. William Whitson), 5:1

[2] Flavius Josephus, *Wars of the Jews* (Philadelphia: Henry Coates & Co., trans. William Whitson), II, 8.1

[3] Robert H. Pfeiffer, *History of New Testament Times* (New York: Harper and Brothers, 1959), 57ff

Chapter 6

A Door Opens to the World

Just as the church has been seen in embryo, now the concept of universalism is seen in that same light. The debate waged by Stephen and the Hellenists from some of the Jewish synagogues opened the door to a new responsibility inherent in the message of Jesus. It may seem a bit strange that the universal message Stephen proclaimed seemed to be a "red flag" to the Hellenists with whom he debated. It just may be that those who had lived in the Diaspora were more cognizant of the potential issues that would soon appear.

Acts 6:8 – 7:1

It is interesting that the community was still worshipping in the Jewish institutions, the temple and the synagogues. As yet, there had been no separation or effort to separate the two groups. The accusers of Stephen were from the areas of Diaspora Judaism and were worshippers in what was probably a Hellenistic synagogue. They were from Africa (Cyrene and Alexandria), and some were from what is now known as Asia Minor. The term Asia referred to a Roman province on the western end of what composes modern Turkey. But they were Jews and were worshipping in a synagogue in Jerusalem, meant to serve the Hellenists.

One might expect that Hellenists would be open to the idea of leaving behind the bonds of Jewish nationalism and offering the message of the gospel to Gentiles, but these were not. (It is probably correct that some of the Hellenist Christians would have understood the broader message, but some may not have been persuaded, and certainly the non-Christian Jews would not have been open to the idea.) Perhaps the exclusiveness that reached back to the time of Ezra's messages prevented them from accepting Gentiles unless they became proselytes. One can easily sympathize with Ezra and the issues he faced when he returned to the homeland, but the ensuing attitude seemed to forget the portion of the promise to Abraham indicating that he was to be a blessing to the whole world. Apparently the charges brought against Stephen were a warped misunderstanding of what Stephen said, but in a sense they proved to be accurate. Barriers were beginning to break down, mountains were being moved, and the fears of conservatism caused them to counter his approach. Stephen's response, or defense if one wishes to call it that, undercut the Hellenists' arguments. (This speech is often called an apology, but the term in theological discussions simply means an explanation.)

Acts 7:2-8:1

This speech of Stephen's was designed to accomplish several things. It was, first of all, a beautiful, abbreviated narrative of some of the history of Israel. But Stephen became the link between the movement being just another Jewish sect and having a world-wide mission. It is entirely possible that the influence of Stephen can be connected closely with the thought pattern in the book of Hebrews. There is good reason to suspect that a type of Jewish/Alexandrian thought became influential in a rather unique understanding about the person and mission of Jesus and the responsibility of followers to reach out beyond Judaism.[1]

The Jews had developed the concept that somehow God dwelt in and was tied to the land. When they were in captivity, Daniel and others opened windows toward Jerusalem in order to pray. (The book of Daniel is set in the framework of the captivity, but was probably written because of the problems encountered during the rampage of Antiochus Epiphanes around 167 B.C.E.) In his speech, Stephen showed that the land was not necessary. God first appeared to Abraham outside of the land while he was in Chaldea, and Abraham did not actually own any of that land except a cave that he bought for burial. (Stephen said, "Not even a foot's length.") God also dealt with Moses while he was in a foreign land, long before the law and the temple. Stephen stated that God did not and does not dwell in temples made with human hands. All of those things (the land, the law, the priesthood, and the holy place) were not necessary for worship. So everything about their understanding of the covenant relationship was questioned. *None of those things was the basis for or essential to worship.* The false witnesses and others were unable to counter Stephen's logic, so they charged him with blasphemy against Moses and God, and against the Holy Place. This led to the stoning of Stephen. Often, when logic cannot prevail, anger does. When Stephen claimed to have seen the "Son of Man" at the right hand of God, it was more than they would allow. Consequently, the execution appears to have risen out of anger. Since the whole narrative deals with the council, it may be correct to say that the Sanhedrin was responsible, but also it may have been a situation that got out of hand because of hatred and frustration. That they "ground their teeth" at him would seem to imply uncontrollable anger. Some accounts suggest that in a formal stoning, the victim was forced to kneel while a large stone was dropped on his or her head. Such an act would probably render the victim unconscious, but Stephen was conscious for some time. A side note in Luke's account, which proved ultimately to have been of immeasurable value, was that their garments were piled at the feet of Saul and that he witnessed all of this, probably even Stephen's last prayer. Saul approved of the killing.

It would be impossible to know whether all of those involved in the stoning were outside the Christian group. The debate began with the Hellenistic Jews and could have included some of the Christian group. Was this persecution an external one, or could it have also been internal? One cannot help but wonder why the Hebrew wing of the church led by the apostles escaped this wrath. It might be because Stephen represented a completely different thought regarding the mission with which they might not have agreed. Notice that in the following verses the apostles escaped the "scattering." Why? But although it would be a long time falling, another barrier had been confronted.

However the persecution might have started and however difficult it may have been, it created a positive outcome, for the church in Jerusalem was scattered throughout Judea and Samaria. (Notice again: "except for the apostles.") Much of the terror exercised against the group was led by the young rabbi, Saul, who was described as "ravaging the church." That term suggests the savagery with which he was going about the task. It was more than just destroying the church; it was like a dog continuing to shake a rat he has caught and killed. Saul was wreaking horrible punishment on those he caught, but instead of destroying the church, he spread it much like a globule of mercury when it is hit in the laboratory. It went all over the place in little cells. Events like these may have been the inspiration that later caused Paul to write in Romans 8:28, "For we know that in reference to all things God works cooperatively for good to those who love him, that is, to those who are called according to his purposes." The accusative of *panta* is an accusative of reference, and the verb *sunergei* means "he works in cooperation with."

Some may be hesitant to see the apostles as dragging their feet, but any kind of ingrained prejudice is extremely difficult to overcome, and there is every reason to believe that the forward-thinking element of the church brought about an emphasis with which the apostles were not yet ready to deal. One must simply read between the lines to make a conclusion as to why the apostles were not scattered.

Acts 8:4-25

It is interesting that another of the seven, who also appears to have been a Hellenist, took up the mantle and proceeded to continue Stephen's emphasis. Philip was not sent out as a missionary from the Jerusalem community; he proclaimed the Messiah to the Samaritans on his own authority. Much went on in this encounter that Luke did not tell us about. There were signs and wonders that captured the attention of one, later known as Simon Magus, who had set himself up as someone important by doing things through magic. Just what he had been doing is not said, but when the Samaritan people turned to Philip, it gave Simon cause for concern. He could not do what Philip was doing, and Luke tells us that even Simon believed. That statement, coupled with the later condemnation by Peter, would make one question just what "even Simon believed" entailed.

When the news got back to Jerusalem about these events, Peter and John were sent to Samaria. There are numerous explanations concerning why the Jewish people were so prejudiced against the Samaritans. Some have indicated that when the Jews began to rebuild the temple after their return from captivity, there was a man, Sanballet, who offered to help. His offer was rejected, probably because those returning saw the Samaritans as mixed-breeds and because they felt the Samaritans had not been concerned with rebuilding the temple while the exiles were in Babylon. Thus, in the eyes of the "faithful," the Samaritans would have defiled the new temple. Whatever the causes, the rejection led to the building of a Samaritan temple on Mount Gerizim, which in a sense competed with the one in Jerusalem. It needs to be recognized that for missionaries to go to Samaria was a huge and controversial step for the church. From the account it is evident that, in some sense, Peter and John represented the power of the Holy Spirit, but did not Philip do so as well? It appears more likely that Peter and John were sent to investigate, and when they saw it they gave their approval by the laying on of their hands. From the many issues where this idea is reported, it is evident that the church saw the evidence of the presence of the Holy Spirit a sign of God's approval of the direction the movement was taking. When that sign of approval among the Samaritans occurred, another of the barriers had been partially removed. There is no mention that Simon received the spirit; in fact, since he tried to buy that power, it would imply that he did not. That effort to buy the power of the spirit, which was so repulsive to Peter, later gave the name "simony" to any attempt to buy religious power or position. When one reads the later history of the church, one finds so much bribery and selling of offices and positions by emperors and popes alike that it is easy to see how far the church had moved from its original stand. There is no indication that Peter and John preached as they came to Samaria, but after they had seen all that had taken place under Philip's leadership, they returned to Jerusalem. On their way, they proclaimed the good news to the Samaritans. (Later on, it is a bit shocking that Peter did not use this to show that God had granted repentance to those outside of Judaism.) Overcoming this mountain may have been the beginning of a kind of conversion experience for Peter and John, especially when one later reads of Peter's dealing with Cornelius, a Roman centurion.

Acts 8:26-40

It is difficult to distinguish difference in the phrases "an angel of the Lord" and "the spirit of the Lord." They are each used in this passage and represent the same inspiration and leadership. There may have been no difference at all in the mind of Luke, but the inspiration to go into an area that was desert was certainly seen as directed by God. Philip met a chariot carrying an Ethiopian eunuch, a servant of Queen Candace. This man was a god-fearer, but he was likely denied the privilege of becoming a proselyte because of his physical mutilation. It is recorded in Deuteronomy 23:1 that a eunuch, or anyone else with genital impairment, was banned from the assembly of Israel. That and other prohibitions of handicapped people were described in Leviticus 21:16-23. Even though the prohibition against eunuchs had been abandoned in Isaiah 56:3-5, it did not mean that the Jewish establishment had adopted the practice. This event represents not only the crossing of a racial barrier, but an acceptance into the Christian community of those who have physical impairments.

The opportunity came to Philip when this man, who was on his way back to Ethiopia, was reading from an Isaiah scroll (Isaiah 53:3-5). Because scrolls were scarce, the eunuch having one demonstrates either a real sacrifice for him or an indication of his financial status. That he took it back to Ethiopia along with an understanding of Jesus and the mission probably signals the beginning of the Coptic church. This Isaiah passage was used by the rabbis as a messianic prophecy, but it was applied to the nation rather than to an individual. Early on, the Christian community saw these "servant poems" in Isaiah as messianic and referring to Jesus.

The gradual abandonment of the messianic interpretations by Jewish writers was no doubt due to the Christian application of the message to Jesus. According to H. Loewe, it was for the same reason that Isaiah 52:13-53:12 was not included in the Haphtaroth or public reading from the prophets, although the passages immediately preceding and following were included.[2]

So when Philip asked the eunuch if he understood the passage, it provided the perfect opportunity to introduce the message about Jesus. The eunuch responded and was baptized. The eunuch raised an interesting question which may have reflected his disappointment that he had been semi-ostracized from the full worship that the Hebrews enjoyed. That question will also arise later when Peter is defending himself in regard to entering the house of Cornelius (Acts 11:17). In both instances, Luke conveys the idea that there was no hindrance by using the same root (*kolu*) as the adverb that closes Acts. Verse 37, "And Philip said, "If you believe with all of your heart, you may." And he replied, "I believe that Jesus Christ is the Son of God," is not in the better manuscripts. Perhaps that represents a later Christian confession that was inserted in later documents.

The translation, "Philip was snatched away," should probably be translated, "Philip was taken away." It does not require a sudden and immediate snatching away of Philip, like some modern science-fiction idea of "beam me up." Luke clearly meant to show that the departure was directed by the Spirit. Philip is found next at Azotus, and as he passed through the region he proclaimed the good news and then went to Caesarea.

[1]William Manson, *The Epistle to the Hebrews* (London: Hodder and Stoughton, Ltd.,1953), 25-26.

[2]F.F. Bruce, *The Acts of the Apostles* (Aberdeen: The University Press, 1953), 193.

Chapter 7

A New Instrument for the Living Lord

It is not possible to know all of the factors that entered into Saul's spiritual struggle. What went through his mind as he saw the stoning of Stephen and heard the confessions of the man and his prayer of concern for those who killed him? Many visions, dreams, and spiritual inspirations may be triggered by events that one experiences. God can use many things to bring about conviction and change, some known and some unknown, but nothing God does among his people occurs in a vacuum. In one of his accountings of his conversion, Saul mentions the shedding of Stephen's blood.

Only a short summary will be offered here, although hours could be spent looking into Saul's background and a great many works have examined it. We know from his own statements that he was from the city of Tarsus, a large metropolis in Cilicia and the western capital of Syria. The city was bounded on the north by the Taurus Mountains and on the east by the Amanus Mountains. It lay in a fertile and luxuriant plain, and because of its topography/geography the area was plagued by malaria. The Cydnus River flowed through the city, and its source was in the mountains. It was a short river and navigable, but extremely cold. On one occasion, Cleopatra's ship docked at the city, which is only about three-fourths of a mile from the sea. One of the great Roman roads running from Ephesus to Antioch in Syria passed through Tarsus. It appears to have been an extremely wealthy trade center and was one of the world's principle seats of Stoic philosophy.

Saul's family was most probably originally from Galilee, the city of Gischala. In the fourth century C.E., a tradition was prominent that the family moved to Tarsus around the time of the death of Herod the Great. They seem to have been financially comfortable and to have cherished Roman citizenship. Saul had been born a Roman citizen (Acts 22:28), and several theories have been advanced to explain that citizenship, none of them proved. In 63 B.C.E., the Roman general

Pompey conquered Palestine and took some Jewish captives to Rome. Those were later manumitted and granted Roman citizenship, and if they so wished they were allowed to return to their own countries, or perhaps live wherever they wished. Others have suggested that the citizenship was an honorary endowment bestowed by the Romans for some unknown deed.[1] Still others have proposed that the family might have been placed there by the Seleucid ruler, Antiochus Epiphanes (175-164 B.C.E.), and given full rights.[2] How Saul gained the citizenship is not important for this study. According to his own statement, he belonged to the Pharisee sect and was from the tribe of Benjamin. He had been trained as a rabbi, most likely under the great Gamaliel, whose testimony had been responsible for gaining some measure of relief for the apostles. As was true of all rabbis, Saul had learned a trade so that he could support himself; his was tent making. He must have been a member of the Sanhedrin because he cast his vote against the saints who were being condemned to death (Acts 26:10). That would shed some light on his personal status, for it was considered a responsibility that every Jewish man should marry, but more than that, it was required that members of the Sanhedrin should be married and have at least one child. Of course, when he is found in Acts, he is alone. There might have been some bitterness if his wife had left him when he became a follower of Jesus. Many things must have transpired when he was converted, not the least of which might have been a negative response from his family. Regardless, the only reference to his family had to do with a nephew, the son of his sister.[3]

Saul's normal Jewish training would have taken place in the "House of Book," where he would have learned both Hebrew and Aramaic. But since he lived in Tarsus, he also would have been fluent in Greek. He probably learned the Old Testament by oral repetition. It would be a mistake to assert that he did not know Stoic philosophy, since Tarsus was famous for its Stoic schools. Anyone who studies him finds evidence that he was an inquisitive learner, and there are, at times, references that appear to follow Stoic thinking.

This early account of his conversion is the first of three in the book of Acts. It must have occurred shortly after the stoning of Stephen and during the intense persecution of the church. Saul is described as initiating the journey to Damascus by going to the high priest and asking for authorization papers so that he could bring any who belonged to the "Way" back to Jerusalem, presumably for proper punishment. Such permission had been granted to the Sanhedrin by the Romans during the rule of Simon as high priest (I Maccabees 15:15-21). That decree was probably still in effect.

Acts 9:1-19

The intensity with which Saul went about carrying out his responsibilities is consistent with the kind of character he demonstrated during his Christian ministry. There can be little doubt that Saul encountered the risen Lord on his way to Damascus. The story is told three times (here and in Acts 22 and 26), and Saul refers to the experience several other times. Something extraordinary had to occur to interrupt him from his mission and transform him into the prime proponent of the movement he had been determined to destroy. By his own admission, there is evidence that he thought he was doing what God wanted in trying to wipe out the movement. The encounter is described as a brilliant light flashing around him and some sort of noise. That, to him, was the direct challenge from Jesus. There is some confusion in the English translations of the three narratives in regard to what those who were with him heard. The account in Acts 9 states that they also heard a voice, but saw no one. The account in Acts 22:9 states that they did not hear the voice. Greek grammar may help to clarify the apparent discrepancy. Most certainly, Luke, who was a native to the Greek language, knew the fine distinctions that could be expressed and would never have written something that was contradictory.

In the first account (9:7), the participle is used with the genitive case and states that they "heard the voice but saw no one." It does not imply any understanding, only that they heard some kind of noise. In the second account (22:9), the accusative case is used, which usually implies some understanding of the content. These two statements should be translated, "they heard a sound" (9:7) and "they did not understand" (22:9). The final account, in Acts 25, does not refer to those with Saul.

> "The Accusative Case (case of extent) accents the intellectual apprehension of the sound, while the Genitive Case (specifying case) calls attention to the sound of the voice without accenting the sense. The word *akouo* itself has two senses which fall well with this case distinction, one 'to hear' the other 'to understand'."[4]

The first account of Saul's conversion does not expand much on what instructions he received, but the statement "I am Jesus whom you are persecuting" must be examined. As far as can be determined by the narratives, Saul never laid a hand on Jesus, yet here he is charged with having persecuted him. That may help to account for the later theology in which Saul/Paul used the phrase "Christ in you" and "Christ lives in me" (Galatians 2:20), or even that the early church was considered "the Body of Christ," which would mean that whenever he persecuted any of the followers of Jesus, he, in fact, had been persecuting Jesus himself. There is a second thought stated in the last of these accounts: "Saul, Saul, why are you persecuting me. It hurts you to kick against the goads." (Acts 26:14) That statement has been assimilated into some of the late manuscripts of this account (9:7), but it is not in the more reliable ones. Could it be that the memory of all that happened to Stephen lodged in Saul's mind and goaded him constantly? So often, even insignificant encounters may have permanent and dramatic impact. For a short period, Saul was blinded by the intense light; there may have been permanent damage. While he talked about "his thorn in the flesh," he never indicated what it actually was. We have evidence in the book of Galatians (6:1) that he did have some eye problems. So even when "something like scales" fell from his eyes and he was able to see again, there may have been some residual damage.

Acts 9:19-25

The disciple, Ananias of Damascus, was reluctant to go to Saul, and who could blame him? What Ananias had heard about Saul during the three days before he went to him, we can never know. But he felt compelled by the Spirit to help, and the result was a marvelous, dramatic transformation. Perhaps the most immediate of the early problems that had faced the early church was solved; the once zealous persecutor had become a follower. *What a mountain to move.* As has been the case throughout the record of biblical revelation, when there has been a need, it seems that God always has a person to meet that need. In the following discussions, it will be evident that Saul was that person. His previous ability, knowledge, tenacious spirit, and rabbinical training could all now be utilized to show that Jesus was indeed the Christ. Saul was to become the standard bearer to those outside Judaism. It should not be surprising that the very Jews with whom he had been closely associated now found him to be a formidable opponent as he reasoned with them in their synagogue to show that Jesus was the son of God. They found no way to rid themselves of this traitor other than to kill him. The disciples in Damascus, who were both frightened about a possible "fifth columnist" and astounded at what seemed to have taken place, helped him to flee by lowering him outside the city wall in a basket. Acts does not mention it, but in Galatians 1:15-18, Saul writes that he was in Arabia for approximately three years. Anyone who has struggled with becoming convinced of a different theological position knows that such a radical change would necessitate a time of re-orienting his entire theological understanding. This may be why he made the journey immediately after his escape from Damascus.

Acts 9: 26-31

Because they knew how viciously Saul had tried to destroy the community wherever he found it, the disciples were skeptical. If this were not real but a trick, it would be a perfect way to discover others who were a part of the church. Many of the people in the early church were probably not certain of Saul's conversion. They may have even doubted that God could bring about such a change. There are several places in the New Testament where the character of Barnabas is shown to fit the nickname they had given him, "Son of Consolation," and this is one of them. When others were afraid, he took Saul and vouched for the experiences that he had been involved in on the road to Damascus, and with Ananias, and with others we may not know. But what an addition to the missionary force Saul could be — a man able in theology and in rabbinical background who could use all of his knowledge to proclaim the truth about Jesus. The message of Saul appears to have aroused the same enemies that Stephen had, but perhaps even more so because the opponents of the movement were unable to match Saul's wisdom and training. And so they resorted to attempting to annihilate him. It is to the credit of the believers in Jerusalem that they protected him and sent him to Tarsus. Another barrier had fallen, perhaps the most serious external one so far, but the gospel moved on, unhindered. For a short time the church had peace from external enemies, and it continued to increase.

Acts 9:32-43

The miraculous events that accompanied the work of the apostles are told to show that the spirit of Jesus was working. The healing of Aeneas demonstrated the power of Christ. There is some distinction to be made between the people restored to life and the resurrection of Jesus. The restorations of Lazarus, the widow's son at Nain, the daughter of Jairus, and this one dealing with Dorcas are not of the same nature as the resurrection of Jesus. In each of the cases mentioned, the same body is reported to have regained life. This was not the case with Jesus, who is called by Saint Paul "the first born from the dead" (Colossians 1:18). Jesus' resurrection body, while retaining some continuity, was also different. Although nothing is said about any of those restored to life, it is reasonable to suppose that they would have to die again, which is certainly not the case with Jesus. While these were remarkable occurrences and they persuaded some to believe, they did not approach the significance of the resurrection of Jesus. Peter's experiences were still within the community of Jewish Christians, but Peter was being led, step by step, to an incredulous new and broader understanding of the Christian mission. Already some progress had been made. He did go to Samaria and recognized the work of the Holy Spirit there, but those people were not "pure" Gentiles. The steps were small, but they were hard to make. Yet some, following the impact of the message of Stephen, had baptized Gentiles (the eunuch), and some from Cyprus and Cyrene had spoken to Hellenists or Greeks (Acts 11:20). This is all part of the story of how the gospel conquered the religious and cultural mountains and started the process of bringing about Gentile inclusion. One further example in regard to Peter's education: while he was in Joppa, he stayed in the home of Simon, the tanner. Simon's occupation involved handling carcasses and hides and would have probably rendered him unclean and his house unfit for a good Jew to enter. At this point, Perter seems to have gotten beyond that ceremonial defilement. Perhaps there was a continual nagging in the consciences of the apostles about all ceremonial cleansing. It is from Mark 7:19 that we learn that Jesus, at one point, cleansed all foods, and the source of Mark's gospel was most likely the preaching of Peter. It must be true that either Peter remembered the story, or else the tradition included it after the church had made the radical move to include Gentiles. So perhaps for Peter, living in those conditions may have contributed to his vision and the instruction not to consider anything that God had cleansed as unclean.

[1] Frank Stagg, *The Book of Acts* (Nashville: Broadman Press, 1955), 110.
[2] David Smith, *The Life and Letters of Saint Paul* (New York: Harper and Brothers, 1950), 19, 20.
[3] Smith, *The Life and Letters*, 30, 31.
[4] A.T. Robertson, *A Manual Grammar of the Greek New Testament in the Light of Historical Research* (Nashville: Broadman Press, 1934), 506.

Chapter 8

A Giant Step Forward

Acts 10:1-33

To those who may have trouble believing that God works in mysterious ways, this story may seem far out, but who knows how God works? Peter had already made some progress toward a different understanding of inclusiveness, as shown by his preaching in Samaria and in the coastal cities, and he had stayed with a family whose ritualistic cleanliness could be questioned. There must have been many things going through his mind regarding this new and puzzling direction. Formerly, proselytes had been admitted to the church, and while the eunuch, to whom Philip had preached and administered baptism, probably went back to Ethiopia and was not a constant reminder of the issue between himself and the Jerusalem community, it had been a departure. Peter, along with John, had been involved in dealing with the Samaritans, but Luke now moves the story to include a God-fearing Gentile (Roman), and a principle is discovered that is new to Peter; that is, "God does not receive man according to his face." Yet such a discovery is fraught with difficulty. What is to be the relationship between Jews and Gentiles in the unity of the Christian Church? Are they to eat together? Is that contaminating? Does one also have to recognize that it is necessary to determine what the relationship of these new converts is to the body? That issue was plagued with problems, certainly to the Jewish wing of the church, and it would take years to decide it.

The story clearly indicated that Peter was hungry and that while waiting for breakfast he "fell into a trance." Exactly what that meant or what entered into the making of the vision is hard to say, but it would appear that there was something of meaning to Peter regarding the various kinds of animals. Some were clean and some were not. Those unclean meats were forbidden by Jewish law, and Peter's conscience would not permit him to eat. Then came the forward-looking revelation declaring that some things that were called unclean were, in fact, clean. When the gospel of Mark was written some thirty years later, this principle was interpreted to have been what Jesus did in cleansing all foods. Perhaps that interpretation was one of Peter's contributions to Mark's account, but what was learned at this time was that it applied to more than food. The vision disappeared and, according to Luke's account, Peter was puzzled about what the vision could mean. While Peter was trying to make sense of it, Cornelius' messengers came to the house, at which time Peter must have realized that people other than Jews were not to be considered as unclean.

Cornelius was a Roman centurion of the Italian Cohort. Roman legions were composed of 6,000 men, and each legion had ten cohorts. That would mean that Cornelius was in command of one of the "centuries" (100 men) that made up the Italian Cohort. A centurion was something like a warrant officer; he was the highest of what we might call non-commissioned officers or, perhaps, even a low-level commissioned one. There is evidence that many centurions were highly respected by the Jews. Some may have provided money to build synagogues.

Cornelius was not a proselyte, just a devout man seeking God. He lived in the city of Caesarea, which had been named for Caesar Augustus, who was emperor from about 38 B.C.E. until 12/14 C.E. Augustus had given the title "King" to Herod the Great, and in turn Herod had honored him by building the city in Greek style and naming it "Caesarea." It had a temple containing images of the emperor. It was a garrison city, and the procurator lived there. Herod had also built an artificial harbor, an engineering marvel of that time. It does not seem that the Roman military offered any interference with the personal religious choices of the occupying soldiers.

Cornelius had received a vision. While going about his religious duties at the hour of prayer, around 3 p.m., he became aware that he had received favor with God regardless of his race, his lack of access to the temple, and other religious necessities, as the Jews understood it. He was directed to send for Peter, who was in Joppa, about thirty miles from Caesarea. Timewise, his vision coincided with the one that Peter had experienced.

One is again reminded that Jesus had stated that all things were clean (see above), but while that statement had probably been preserved orally, it had not been written and probably not understood at the time of these visions. This is a major mountain to overcome. There were those in the church, especially in Jerusalem, who observed the prohibitions in Leviticus 11. As has already been hinted, one must now consider whether it is possible for Jews in the church to remain aloof from Gentiles, if they were allowed at all. (From the gospel story it would appear that one of the things that irritated Jesus was the way that people were divided into classes, especially by the Jewish religious system.) If Gentiles are to be allowed in, does that mean that all people can disregard the provisions of the law relative to clean and unclean? It was a complicated and sensitive issue. Perhaps to try to get some feel of the tension, we need to think of a modern issue that divides Christians. There are many sincere, stalwart followers of Christ who have been upset by the homosexuality issue. Issues that are intensely emotional can create deep divisions, even though there may be convincing arguments, pro or con.

The party sent by Cornelius appeared in the street, asking for Peter, who wanted to know why they were seeking him and what they wanted. Then, as they spoke about Cornelius (who fell into the category of "God-fearer"), Peter put his vision and the arrival of the men together and learned a tremendous, but dangerous lesson. He provided hospitality for them and later went with them to Caesarea. It had been suggested to Peter that he should go without hesitation, but he had to have known the underlying issues and what he would have to face. It was somewhat as personal protection that he took six witnesses with him. (Jewish law demanded only two witnesses.) As we look back on it, Peter's interpretation of the vision was obviously correct. But Peter was still a good Jew, as is shown by his statement that it was unlawful for a Jew to fraternize with any Gentile. Was this a special case? When he heard Cornelius' half of the vision and saw the attitude of the messengers, he went with them to Caesarea.

Cornelius met with Peter with an attitude that was a bit surprising for an occupying military man to have toward a native. It was, however, an attitude of respect and worship, and he had to be reminded that Peter was only a mortal. In spite of the vision, Peter stated, almost apologetically, that he had some problem going into the house of a Gentile. Rarely do people understand that prejudice works from both sides of racial barriers, and apparently it did not occur to Peter that Cornelius might have had some of the same issues with him. Exclusiveness and prejudice always involve an attitude of superiority, and both the Romans and the Jews had that barrier. How could it be eliminated?

Any serious reader of this story must remember that the narrative was written nearly forty years after the event. It is much easier to deal with history after the event than to participate in it. Peter knew that most of the Jerusalem church would not look kindly on what he was doing and that going to the Gentiles was becoming a major problem. For a reader in the United States, consider how difficult it was during the civil rights movement of the 1960s to take a stand on racial equality when the accepted position, even by many religious leaders, was "separate but equal." Even with the protection of the United States Constitution, it was not easy to go against the grain.

Acts 10:34-48

Whether we have the complete message that Peter proclaimed to Cornelius and those gathered with him, it was a short outline of the *kerygma*. It also contained the interesting lesson Peter had learned, literally "God is not one who receives personal appearance." It is of note that he did not lay the blame on the Romans or emphasize their part in the death of Jesus. But at this point, an important change happened in regard to these Gentiles. While Peter was speaking, the Holy Spirit came upon those who were listening. One must remember that even in Samaria, the Holy Spirit was not evident until after people had been baptized and Peter and John laid hands on them. Why was the order so different this time? Peter and those with him may still have been perplexed about what to do, and such evidence of God's approval would convince them that Gentiles also should be baptized and become part of the fellowship. That is a radical departure, and it took compelling evidence to convince them and gain their willing approval. (This is something like when those of us who interpret Peter's use of Joel in the Pentecost sermon now say, "We did not say this event began the last days. Peter said it."). Later, in defense of his action, Peter could say, "I did not authorize the baptism of Gentiles. The Spirit did." It should also be noted that Philip did not hesitate to baptize the eunuch, perhaps because he had already come to such a dominant perspective regarding Stephen's message of universalism. It was people like Stephen who forced the Jewish segment of the church to accept Gentiles.

This is, at least to this point in the narrative, the most astounding development in the church's coming to grips with the increasing effort to reach out to the world. In some ways, Peter went "kicking and screaming" in following the leadership of the Holy Spirit, but it is to his credit that he did go. Later, this event would provide one of the great arguments in trying to settle the issue of the Gentiles and what to do with them. We should remind ourselves of the many ministers who strongly supported slavery in the United States and even found scriptural passages to bolster that support. It is also interesting that in telling the story of the eunuch and of the conversion of Cornelius and his people, Luke indicated that nothing *hindered* the baptism.

Acts 11:1-18

If it is correct that Luke was attempting to show how the good news spread, regardless of the internal and external opposition that the movement brought (here is the term "hinder" again in verse 17), it is not surprising that almost before the visit to Cornelius had been completed, the news got back to Jerusalem, and there were those who were upset by Peter's action. The church had previously confronted selfishness and greed, which threatened the spirit of *koinonia*. It had also weathered external storms of persecution when the Sanhedrin attempted to rid itself of the blame for the death of Jesus, actual imprisonments, and who knows what else? These incidents had been prompted by the Jewish priestly group who had authorized Saul to "ravage" the church, and by the marvelous conversion of Saul and the opposition created against him. Now Peter, one of their own leaders, had proclaimed the gospel to Gentiles who were right in their midst. What was next?

So Peter, one of the original disciples, was called on the carpet before the circumcision party of the Jerusalem community and asked, in what must have been a hyper-critical and accusing way, "Why did you do a thing like this, going to those who were uncircumcised and even eating with them?" It had not been mentioned before that there was a circumcision party, except for an implication that there was such a division in the passing problem with the Hellenistic widows. The issue was obviously present and would become the major conflict in the remainder of Luke's story.

> "It is clear that the Jerusalem Christians were very conservative. When Peter returned to Jerusalem, the circumcision party taxed him with having entered a Gentile house and eaten with its occupants. (v.3) They do not fasten the baptism of the Gentiles as the main crime, and curiously enough, Peter does not refer to this matter in his defense. He just tells the whole story (Luke abbreviates it for literary effect) and refers to the well-known saying of John the Baptist, to the effect that the Messiah would not baptize with water, but with the Holy Spirit. According to this account the Jerusalem Christians accepted the situation, perhaps with a tinge of regret, 'Then hath God also to the Gentiles granted repentance unto life.' They continued to make difficulties, but these were the terms on which Gentiles would be admitted to the church, and on subsequent relations with them, rather than on the question of admission itself." (See Acts 15:1-28 and Galatians 2:11-14.)[1]

Peter simply defended himself by describing the peculiar visions he and Cornelius had experienced. But the major thrust of his defense was that the Holy Spirit had apparently approved of the visit even *before* he extended a call for repentance, because the Spirit fell on the Gentiles unexpectedly. Peter also indicated that he had sufficient witnesses (six of them) who not only went with him to Caesarea, but were also present when he confronted the circumcision party. That the Spirit came on these people before they were baptized most assuredly indicated approval of this progress. Of course, Jesus had told them that they would be responsible for going into all the world, but so often elements of a message like that (and even that the Messiah would be a "suffering servant") were hard to digest. So who was Peter to hinder God? A bit later in the narrative, at the Jerusalem Conference, Peter said, "In fact, we believe that it is through the grace of the Lord Jesus *that we are saved in the same manner as they are*" (Acts 15:11, author's emphasis). It almost appears that since the theological battle was not over, their acquiescence meant something like, "This is a unique case, and in it God has given, for this time, repentance to these particular Gentiles." Therefore, it was a special case and demanded acceptance even by those who would later come to be known as "Judaizers."

[1] R.R. Williams, *The Acts of the Apostles* (London: SCM Press Ltd., 1956), 94

Chapter 9

The Center Shifts

Acts 11:19-30

Luke's narrative now returned to the persecution that arose over Stephen's preaching. Many had scattered to spread the message in the coastal area of Phoenicia, to the island of Cyprus, and to Antioch in Syria. To begin they spoke only to Jews, but some who were most likely natives of Cyprus and Cyrene spoke also to Greeks. There is a textual problem in this verse which indicates that they either spoke to the "Hellenists" (*Hellenistas*) or to the Greeks (*Hellenas*). While the manuscript evidence heavily supports the term "Hellenists," the entire thrust of the passage seems to focus on the Gentiles. The following translations or paraphrases are samples of those who either render the term as "Greeks" or "Gentiles." (Beck, N*ew International Version, The New English Bible; The Good News for Modern Man,* Phillips and Williams) Since the emphasis in Acts seems to be the movement toward the Gentiles, the term *Hellenas*, which would have included Gentiles, may be more accurate.

Once again, when the news came to the church at Jerusalem, the reaction was to send someone to investigate this phenomenon. A more appropriate and sympathetic person than Barnabas could not have been found. He always seems to have been interested in moving the gospel forward rather than promoting himself. One is reminded of the statement of John the Baptist regarding Jesus, "He must increase, but I must decrease." Great servants always demonstrate that spirit.

At this point, Barnabas remembered that Saul had been sent to Tarsus for his own safety, and since Antioch in Syria was not far from Tarsus, Barnabas went there and brought Saul to Antioch. When Barnabas had seen what was taking place, he knew immediately that someone with ability and preparation greater than his own was needed to instruct the new converts in Antioch. The need for qualified instruction would be magnified as the message of the church expanded among non-Jewish persona. That would mean that Barnabas deserves much more of the credit for moving into the Gentile world than we have usually given him, probably because he seemed less important than Saul/Paul, even though he was of the Jerusalem community. Wherever the story was told, the people who received it had no access to written materials such as the gospels. At this point in the history of the movement, there was nothing but oral tradition. There will probably always be a debate about the nature of the "Q" source and other materials, but they appear to have been transmitted orally for some period of time. Even though it has been said before, it needs to be repeated that the oral method of transmission was extremely reliable. It was recorded in the earliest chapters of Acts that the church had continued in the teaching (didache') of the apostles. They were the ones who had been closest to Jesus and who were participants in the events. Therefore, they became the nucleus for the preservation of, and perhaps the explanation of, the materials. When the movement reached outside the Jewish community, new needs arose. Most of the new converts were unfamiliar with Jewish backgrounds and history and had to be taught. There was no effort at this time to sever the message from the Old Testament; rather, it became extremely important that the ties be maintained and strengthened, particularly using the later prophets and the Psalms. While Saul had not been a participant in the early events, it is obvious that he took time to learn them and to interpret then in the light of his rabbinic background. For at least a year, there must have been learning sessions for the converts in Antioch, where the name "Christian" was first applied to them. Some have thought that the term may have been first applied in a derisive way, but it could have been a self-designation, a badge of honor. Again, it must be kept in mind that all of the earliest followers were Jews and all of the apostles were Jews, and the character of the church at Jerusalem reflects that Jewish devotion. In all probability, most, if not all, of those followers believed that the new movement, "The Way," was an extension or continuation of Judaism — indeed, the direction that Judaism should take. It should not be unexpected that some things out of the ordinary had to occur before the movement would reach out to non-Jews. The early believers were attempting to "find their way," and gradually they were led to see the broader picture. There were many Jewish leaders who did not see or were fearful of the broader visions. Vigorous arguments would soon erupt over the issue of including Gentiles.

It should be added that sometime during the early centuries, the idea emerged that the Jews killed Jesus, which is a far cry from what actually happened. The crucifixion occurred because a small group of Jewish leaders who collaborated with the Romans to keep their political position, primarily the high priest and others of the priesthood who were influential in the Sanhedrin, saw clearly the threat in this new movement. They feared this new type of Judaism, largely because of the political dangers which seemed to be developing. Caiaphas' statement that it was good for one man to die and that the whole nation not perish shows some of those religious and political fears. Perhaps one contributing factor was the nationalistic interpretation of the "kingdom." As that issue grew, the conflict became more severe. Soon the believers would divide into two camps, those who understood this movement to be a kind of reform of Judaism and those who believed it was a completely different approach because it was inclusive of all people. That issue was certainly not an easy hurdle to overcome, and it ultimately produced harsh understandings relative to the Jews. As the gospel followers became more and more characterized by "Gentiles," the differences were accentuated. In fact, Saul of Tarsus will later call some of those who opposed him "dogs." That does not indicate that the Judaizers were in some sense servants of and devoted to evil as much as it shows the harshness that was almost inevitable between those who had strong Jewish feelings and were certain that their approach was correct and in keeping with God's will, and those who saw the broader picture.

At this point, it is evident that "orders" were developing in the early church. First there were "apostles," and now we hear of "prophets" and "elders." As of this time, there has been no evidence of a continued order of "deacons." Such groups came about as the organization of the church developed. They were not necessarily "sacred" appointments, but groups that met natural needs. Much later, "monks," "nuns," and others are found. The appearance of Agabas, along with some other prophets from Jerusalem, may represent another phase in the growth of the Jerusalem community. The word prophet is derived from the terms "pro" and "phemi," and it primarily means one who speaks forth the message of God. While there were occasions, such as this one, where predictions were made, that was not the primary prophetic function.

This event may also indicate that the Jerusalem church was not strong financially. Perhaps the early condition of sharing had rendered it economically poor, and the threat of famine required help. A famine, such as the one described, occurred during the reign of Claudius Caesar (41-54 C.E.). It will be seen later that an appropriate chronology can be constructed from the appearance of Gallio in Corinth in 51 C.E. That event can he historically verified and, therefore, some of the events can be dated. If we use the normal suggestion that the crucifixion occurred around 30/31 C.E. and try to construct some order of events from there, and if the Jerusalem Conference (recorded in Acts 15) took place in

49 C.E., we may move backwards to approximate the beginning of what we call the first missionary journey in 46 C.E. Since the reign of Claudius began in 41 C.E., the famine must have occurred about 43/44 C.E.

The spirit of sharing in the church at Antioch demonstrated that whatever the attitude of the Jerusalem church, the people of Antioch recognized the unity of the body and wished to help those in need. The first understanding of caring for the poor likely dealt with those in the community. It should be noted that this was a voluntary gift "according to their ability" and it bears resemblance to the earlier "having all things in common." The attitude in the Jerusalem church was no hindrance to the Christian love from Antioch. That love, the insight of Barnabas and Saul, and guidance from above brought about a shift in what would be the focal center of the movement. The Jerusalem church maintained an important position, largely because of the apostles, but the power of the new, forward-looking position had found a fresh location in the attitude and missionary spirit which the church in Antioch sensed.

Internal barriers were being broken down. Now Luke turned to another external issue, the death of James. This represents the third of the external mountains, and this one comes from the political realm.

Acts 12:1-19

Herod Agrippa I was the son of Aristobulus and the grandson of Herod the Great, who executed Aristobulus in 7 B.C.E. Herod Agrippa I stood in good graces with the Emperor Caligula (37-41 C.E.) because of a remark he made which was overheard by Tiberius that suggested that the empire would be better off when Tiberius died. Agrippa I was imprisoned because of that remark, and when Caligula became emperor at the death of Tiberius, he was released and given the title of king over the Tetrarchy of Philip. Later, when Antipas died in 39 C.E., Galilee and Perea were added to Agrippa's territory. He was instrumental in getting the Senate to accept Claudius as successor to Caligula, and as a reward Claudius gave him the territories of Judea and Samaria. At that time Agrippa ruled over the entire kingdom that Herod the Great had controlled. To appease the Jews, Agrippa made several moves. He came to Judea to live, probably in Jerusalem, and made an effort to show that he kept the law by observing the Passover. According to Luke, that seems to have been why he had one of the disciples, James, killed — but the death is barely mentioned. There is a late tradition (between the fourth and seventh centuries C. E.) that John was also killed at this time, but it is neither reliable nor probable. The primary Christian tradition was that John was exiled on the island of Patmos during the reign of Domitian

(81-96 C.E.) and was the author of the Apocalypse. The death of James was apparently due to a political charge, since he was "killed by the sword." Could it be that Agrippa was fearful concerning the preaching of the kingdom, just as his grandfather had been over the birth of the newborn King?

We wonder why Luke passed over the death so swiftly. Perhaps it reflected his own view of death, i.e. that it was relatively unimportant and simply transposed one from this realm to the spirit realm. Perhaps it was due to the expectation of the early return of Jesus. This short reference does remove any possible confusion between the apostle James and James, the brother of Jesus, who became the leader of the Jerusalem church. It is interesting also, as has been alluded to, that the church did not feel any necessity to replace the apostle James.

During the Passover season, Jewish emotions always ran high. The arrest of Peter and the anticipation of his trial must have been another of Agrippa's efforts to capitalize on that emotion and please the Jews who opposed the new movement. Peter was guarded closely around the clock by four soldiers, with two inside the cell and two outside the door. While Peter was in prison, the church was praying for him. The entire process of his deliverance as it is told indicates some confusion. Peter seemed to think that he was dreaming, and the narrative said that he later came to himself. However it occurred, the chains were removed, and Peter followed someone past two doors and into the street for a city block before he realized that he was free. Apparently the soldiers slept through it and did not know what had happened. That Agrippa believed that there was some dereliction of duty can hardly be doubted, because he had the guards arrested and executed.

The story of Peter's appearance at the home of John Mark's mother is intriguing because of the excitement of the servant girl, Rhoda, and because no one believed that Peter could possibly be free. In fact, following a dominant idea of the Pharisees that everyone has a guardian angel, they assumed that it was Peter's angel knocking. When they finally let him in, he related what had happened and indicated that they should inform James, the brother of Jesus. Then Peter went somewhere else. This is not like the confrontation with the Sanhedrin in which Peter and the others went directly to the temple and continued to preach. It was evident that Herod Agrippa was no Sanhedrin and that whatever kind of trial he would have given Peter would have resulted in his death. So Peter wisely left the area. We do not know where he went, but in the narrative he was later found in Caesarea. This experience may have preceded the Cornelius event.

Acts 12:20-25

This account is a rather remarkable story that explains why the persecution by Agrippa ended. If the account Luke gave had been the only narration of the event, it would be assumed that Herod died instantly. It was not at all unusual for the rulers in the Roman Empire to assume and proclaim their own deity, or for the Senate or the people to give it to them. Herod was really a minor official, but this flattery was designed to get a favorable response. To the early church, his death would have been a just reward. Josephus gave another account of his death:.

> "Now when Agrippa had reigned three years over all Judea, he came to the city of Caesarea, which was formerly called Strabo's Tower, and there he exhibited shows in honor of Caesar, upon his being informed that there was a certain festival celebrated to make vows for his safety. At that festival a great multitude was gotten together of principle persons, and such as were of dignity throughout the province. On the second day of the shows, he put on a garment made wholly of silver, and of a contexture truly wonderful, and came to the theater early in the morning, at which time the garment was illuminated by the fresh reflection of the sun's rays upon it. It shone out after a surprising manner and was so resplendent as to spread horror over those who looked intently upon him, and presently those who flattered him called out, one from one place and another from another, (although not for his own good) that he was a god, and they added, 'Be merciful to us; for although we have hitherto reverenced thee only as a man, yet we shall henceforth own thee as superior to mortal nature.' Upon this the King did neither rebuke them or reject their impious flattery. But as he presently afterwards looked up, he saw an owl sitting on a rope over his head, and immediately understood that this bird was a messenger of ill tidings to him, and he fell into deepest sorrow. A severe pain also arose in his belly, and began in the most violent manner. He therefore, looked upon his friends, and said, 'I, whom you call a god, am commanded to depart this life; while Providence reproves the lying words you just now said to me; and I, who was called by you immortal, am immediately to be hurried away by death. But I am bound to accept what Providence allots, as it pleases God; for we have by no means lived ill, but in a splendid and happy manner.' When he had said this his pain became violent. Accordingly, he was carried into the palace, and the rumor went abroad that he would certainly die in a little time. But the multitude sat in

sackcloth with their wives and children, after the law of their country, and besought God for the King's recovery. All places were also full of mourning and lamentation. Now the King rested in a high chamber, and as he saw them lying prostrate on the ground, he could not forebear himself weeping. And when he had been quite worn out by the pain in his belly for five days, he departed this life, being in the fifty-fourth year of his age, and in the seventh year of his reign; for he, reigned four years under Caius Caesar (Caligula), three of them were over Philip's tetrarchy only, and on the fourth he had that of Herod Antipas added to it; he reigned besides those, three years under the reign of Claudius Caesar."[1]

In this period of history, an owl was considered an omen of death. Evidently, this was a common story, for the work of Josephus is usually dated a couple of decades after the date we have assigned to the writing of Acts. Luke used the issue to demonstrate how the gospel moved on in spite of the political persecution, and he interpreted the death of Agrippa as the judgment of God on him for his acceptance of the claim of deity. The cause of the dispute between Herod and the people is not known, but those cities were dependent on the grain fields of Galilee for their sustenance. Therefore it was vital for them to persuade Agrippa to supply them. The Acts narrative implies strongly that they bribed Blastus to gain the audience, but with the death of Herod their immediate concerns were alleviated. Exactly what caused his death remains unknown. Considering the state of medical diagnosis, it could have been a ruptured appendix, which might have been popularly reported as "eaten of worms."

Barnabas and Saul returned to Antioch from Jerusalem about the time of the death of Herod, which would have been about 44 or 45 C.E., and they brought John Mark with them.

---

[1]Josephus, *The Antiquities of the Jews*, trans. by William Whitson (Philadelphia: Henry T. Coates & Co.), XIX, viii, 2.

Chapter 10

An Incredible Advance

It had been brewing on the horizon for several years, and very small steps had been taken by a radical wing of the church. The church at Antioch was of a totally new spirit. Stephen had muddied the waters with his forward-looking sermon, and the persecution that scattered the church at Jerusalem had led to the recognition that God could work among Samaritans. Philip had taken that same message to an Ethiopian God-fearer, a eunuch, and Peter had been led, somewhat against his will at first, to reach out to Cornelius and his people. Now the progressive element in the Antioch church was inspired to make a remarkable stand. None of the previous efforts to reach out to the whole world had been inaugurated and/or authorized by a church. What Luke reported at this stage was a church-authorized mission that would include uncircumcised Gentiles.

Acts 13:1-13

The church at Antioch had apparently been the recipient of an intensive instruction effort led by prophets and teachers. It is intriguing to see the composition of that group: Barnabas was named first and perhaps was the leader, then a man named Simeon. Simeon must have been a black man, for he was nicknamed "Niger," which is the Latin term for black. It is also interesting that the man who was drafted to help Jesus carry the cross was named Simeon and was from Cyrene. (The fourth gospel did not include the story, which was common to the Synoptics, but rather said that Jesus carried the cross by himself, John 19:17.) That Simeon was listed immediately before Lucius, who was from Cyrene, raises the question whether this Simeon could have been the same man. (The name Simeon, or Symeon, is a Hebrew name for which the Greek, Simon, was substituted.) The group was a varied one, even including a member of the court of Herod, and concluded with Saul. Under the direction of the Spirit, the church sent forth the first organized and approved mission effort. There can be different opinions about what the "laying on of hands" meant in this event. There are some who suggest that the prophets and teachers were being given special status, similar to that of the apostles. However, Saul later insisted that he received his apostleship from God rather than from men. It could also correspond to what the church did later in ordaining people to special service. It may also have been similar to what modern groups do when "commissioning" people for a particular task. Whatever all of its implications could have been, it is certain that this was a direct approval of the mission by the Antioch church. (As a sidelight, it may also be seen that while many believe that the term "conservative" is a badge of honor somewhat protecting the "status quo," it may also inhibit progress.)

Acts 13:4-12

Luke clearly intended to demonstrate that this new direction was approved by God. There is no indication that any direction was given to the party about where they were to go, but that they went to Cyprus should be no surprise, since Barnabas was a native of that island and owned property there. This missionary work was not new; some of it had already been done. It was not new in that it involved preaching to Gentiles, which both Peter and Philip, and perhaps some others, had already done. Luke saw this as particularly important because the need was seen by the church at Antioch, which organized and directed the mission. Should that not be the logical outcome of monotheism? As they began their work in Cyprus, they went first to the synagogue, which appears to have been the procedure that was ordinarily followed in the later work, even among the Gentiles. It is also significant that they had John Mark as their "attendant." The term used to describe Mark's responsibilities was *hyperetes*, which was used to designate the interpreter or teaching attendant in synagogues. It suggests that John Mark's primary role was to take new converts and teach them the gospel tradition and backgrounds. That would be a vital and important task as the movement went more and more toward Gentiles, who had no Jewish background. Since there were no written records, teaching had to be done orally.

Sergius Paulus, the proconsul, heard a rumor about what was happening and asked for an audience. The subsequent encounter with Elymas (or Barjesus) presented another barrier to overcome. In the first century, many magicians attached themselves to whatever persons or position of power they could find. Simon Magus had done so with the people of Samaria, and here the attachment is to Sergius Paulus. In the organization of the system of government in the Roman Empire, there were two kinds of provinces. An imperial province was directly under the control of the emperor, and the ruling appointee, called a "procurator," was responsible to the emperor. The provinces that were under the control of and responsible to the Senate were senatorial provinces, and the governor was a "proconsul." Cyprus was a senatorial province.

When Elymas heard what was taking place, he more than likely thought that he was about to lose his influence. As a result, he appears to have attempted to stop the proconsul from hearing the message. Saul rebuked him severely. This particular sign or wonder helped to convince Sergius Paulus of the power and validity of what Saul and Barnabas were proclaiming. Nothing is said about further events or preaching on the island, but their movement from the eastern port of Salamis to the western one of Paphos would suggest a mission across Cyprus.

Acts 13:13-34

As the journey led them to the area known today as Turkey, they landed at Perga. At that point, John Mark left the party and returned to Jerusalem. No explanation is given, but it must have created some major dissension, because it is later obvious that Paul had lost confidence in him and was not willing to give him a second chance. Several possible reasons for his departure have been suggested by scholars. Some have felt that he became homesick — but he had already been away from Jerusalem for some time. Others have thought that he might have been afraid of sickness and hardship, but while that may be more plausible than the "homesick" theory, those fears would have probably shown up much earlier. Still others have suggested that he was love-sick for an unnamed little "brown eyes," but that is mere conjecture. Still others have seen conflicts with Paul as the reason. Paul may not have been the easiest person to get along with, and John Mark may have concluded that he made a mistake in joining the party. But nothing like that stopped him from being willing to join a second mission and, consequently, joining Barnabas on a similar journey. The most plausible reason, to this author, is that he was unable to adjust to the pace of the rapid push toward universalism. He was a Jerusalem Jew, and we do not know whether he had connections with the Jewish wing of the church. But adjusting to dealing with Gentiles and trying to teach them may not have been easy; Mark may have needed a slower pace.

We may properly ask why his departure had such an impact on Paul. Since Mark was the *hyperetes* for the group, his was a tremendously important part of the work. When he left, someone else had to take up that responsibility, because without him the void in the mission was immeasurable. Basic teaching, especially to those who have no background, is absolutely essential for a strong community to develop. Little is said of any work in Perga. It was the capital of the province of Pamphilia and was one of the centers of the worship of Artemis. Apparently, the visitors stayed only a short time and then moved inland to a higher altitude, to the city of Antioch in Pisidia. Evidently, Paul had felt it necessary to move to this location because of some personal weakness, possibly an illness or an eye problem. The party was now moving to the area we call Galatia. In the later letter to the Galatians, Paul indicated that he had some physical issue which was visible (Galatians 4:13-15). Luke now began using the Greek name instead of the Hebrew one. In Antioch in Pisidia, once again they went into the synagogue and, as was the Jewish custom, they were invited to speak. Luke narrated the essence of Paul's sermon. By this time Paul seems to have become the leader of the group, and the sermon follows the *kerygma* model. There was a brief introductory survey of Israel's history, a discussion of the crucifixion and resurrection, an explanation that Jesus was God's promised Savior, and finally an appeal for repentance. Paul used proof texts from the Psalms, and in light of his later emphasis on faith as the thing that frees mankind, he must have introduced the idea to them. There was great interest in what he said, and some believed and followed. Then there was a request that they return and explain further what had been proposed. Some of those hearers may have been converts to Judaism, proselytes.

Acts 13:44-52

It does not appear that the content of Paul's message was what disturbed the Jews in Antioch of Pisidia. What bothered them was that the Gentiles were responding in rather large numbers, for when they saw the crowds, their opposition arose. Once again, the barrier of cultural and religious prejudice threatened to stop the progress, but rather than stopping it, the direction of the momentum changed, and the Gentiles became the central focus of the mission. There is no record of how responsive some of the Jews may have been, but the emphasis is now on the Gentiles. (The quotation that was used for support was from Isaiah 49:6. Luke had repeated the logic of this reference, although he did not actually quote it in the gospel, and would do so later in Acts 26.) The Second-Isaiah section had become the most prominent of the prophetic passages urging the Jewish people toward a wider vision of their responsibilities, but that direction was not pleasing to the religious leaders of the nation. The emphasis that Paul now made was that the Jews had made themselves unworthy of what God was doing because they had rejected the gospel — not that God had rejected them. The Gentiles were overjoyed that this opportunity had come to them.

There was, during this period, a general breakdown of many of the religious systems that had dominated the Roman Empire, and the reception by the Gentiles indicated something of their hunger. Luke used the concept that "as many as believed were destined for eternal life." That is stated after the fact and should never be used as a proof text for the later Calvinistic doctrine of predestination. The normal pattern seems to have been that after people had responded positively to the gospel, it was believed that God had initiated the interest, but that was not to say that before there was any response these people had been destined either way. (For some, this will bring into focus the debate about free will and determinism.)

Those who believed were described by Luke as being destined to eternal life. Those words have been used to teach the doctrine of predestination in a rigorous sense, which they do not necessarily bear. In the first place, Saint Luke is thinking not so much of individuals as of classes — Jews and Gentiles — and among the latter, those who believed and those who did not. Secondly, his phrase contains a double idea, as it is looked at as from the divine or human side. (1) The Greek word translated "ordain" means properly "to set in order," (2) and its primary use was for ordering or marshalling troops in the line of battle, and so stationing them to a post. Now, as the Jews in Corinth "set themselves in array" against the apostles, from the human point of view these Galatians had marshalled themselves with a view to capturing eternal life. It was the will of God that the Galatians should be saved. But this will, with all of the guiding circumstances and grace given, did not take away the power of man to reject, as is shown by the disobedient Jews who had also received the call to eternal life."[1]

But even with the incited riot and persecution "driving Paul and Barnabas out of their territory," the progress of the gospel moved on unhindered.

Acts 14:1-17

It is not possible to know how large the following among the Jewish people in any of these cases may have been. It is fairly evident that the churches in Galatia later had a strong Gentile core, as can be seen in Paul's letter to the Galatians. However, as they left Antioch, the graphic symbol which Jesus had used was employed, and they "shook off the dust from their feet" in protest against them. The city of Antioch was about 100 miles inland from Perga and considerably higher in elevation. When they went from Antioch to Iconium, the distance was about seventy-five miles on the Royal Road, which had been built by Augustus Caesar. Upon their arrival in that city, they followed the traditional practice of going first to the synagogue. The reception appears to have been very positive, and Luke indicates that a great number of both Jews and Greeks became believers. In this instance, we do not have information about what exactly caused the disruption, only that some unbelieving Jews stirred up the division. Some of the people were said to have sided with the apostles.

Originally, the term "apostle" had been reserved for those who were the initial twelve sent out by Jesus, but here Barnabas and Paul were both called apostles. Paul later claimed to have received his apostleship directly from the risen Christ, but no discussion or claim of apostleship in that sense was made for Barnabas. The term "apostle" means one who is sent forth, and since the church in Syrian Antioch had sent them forth, Luke could have easily applied the term to both men. They were able to stay for a considerable time before the opposition erupted. It may be safe to assume that the racial implications stirred the opposition, but in this case the Jews were said to have poisoned the minds of some of the Gentiles against the apostles. Even the rulers and leaders of the city were involved in this persecution, and what appears to have been an incidence of mob violence culminated in an effort to stone them. (Much later, in Ephesus, the concern of the leaders was that if a report of an uproar and violence in the city reached Rome, it would result in severe consequences for the city. That same fear might have convinced the rulers of the city to act against Paul and Barnabas.) When they discovered this plot, Barnabas and Paul fled to Lystra and Derbe.

An interesting apocryphal story relating to Iconium is found in the *Acts of Paul and Thecla*. According to the story, when Paul came to Iconium, he lived in the house of a man named Onesiphorous. The book refers to Paul as being a small man, with meeting eyebrows and a rather large nose. Baldheaded and bowlegged, he was described as strongly built and full of grace, for at times he looked like a man and at times he had the face of an angel. Thecla is said to have overheard the preaching of Paul and become a believer, after which she refused to marry her betrothed, Thamyria. Paul was brought before the proconsul, Castelius, and accused of persuading the woman not to marry. In the narrative, it is said that because of the trumped-up charge, Paul was ordered to be scourged and expelled from the city. Thecla was condemned to be burned. The pyre was prepared and Thecla was put on it, but as they tried to burn her a terrible storm came and quenched the fire. She was also saved from wild animals, and the story claimed that she became a type of female preacher, teacher, and baptizer, perhaps to justify the right of women to teach and baptize. It is also said that she wanted to cut her hair and follow Paul, but he refused that request. We may never know how much truth is in this story, if any, but it is evident that many things contributed to the problems Paul encountered. Imagine the issues that could have erupted if a wife became a Christian and her pagan husband encountered things that could have disturbed his marriage.[2]

Acts 14:8-20

The procedure in Lystra was different from that in the other two cities. No synagogue is mentioned, only an altar to Zeus. The native dialect is called Lycaonian, and while the people could probably speak Greek, in this case they reverted to their native tongue. Their instant conclusion that Paul and Barnabas were Greek gods in human form is not at all surprising. There are numerous stories in ancient literature of people believing that they had been visited in this way. The two gods they singled out were Zeus and Hermes, giving the title of Zeus to Barnabas and Hermes to Paul. (In Roman mythology, they would have corresponded to Jupiter and Mercury.) When it became obvious to Paul and Barnabas that the people were preparing to offer sacrifices, even under the leadership of the priest of Zeus, they immediately protested, and Paul attempted to proclaim to them the offer of salvation. He tried to guide them to the living God, rather than their pagan ones, by showing them the natural blessings they enjoyed. He seems to have suggested that in years gone by, God allowed men to go their own way, and was probably saying that they must leave the past behind and see God in action now in a unique way. However, in places where he alludes to this idea, he always argues that God did not leave himself without a witness. It was in the realm of nature. Luke did not take time in this narrative to show the people's reaction, for the story was interrupted as Jews from Antioch and Iconium came and incited the crowd to stone Paul. The Jews were so opposed to Paul's message that it seems they would prefer to have the natives involved with Zeus rather than with God.

Either way, they were either extremely careless about deciding that Paul was dead, or he had rather remarkable recuperative powers. The next day he traveled about forty miles, probably on foot. But the gospel still moved on, and a small group of believers must have been left behind in each of these towns/cities.

Acts 14: 21-28

It is a credit to Paul and Barnabas and to the way they must have been emboldened by the Spirit that they went back through the very areas where they had been attacked. It would have been an easy overland journey from Derbe to Antioch in Syria, but there was more work to be done. Not only did they find it necessary to offer added strength and instruction for the new disciples, but they saw that some kind of structure was needed in the churches in these towns. Perhaps because of these persecutions there had not been time to do the task that John Mark would have been expected to do. So they appointed elders in each of the churches and entrusted them unto the Lord. Nothing is said about the specific tasks they expected the elders to perform, but some authority or leadership was necessary. Perhaps they instituted a "crash course" in the tradition before they left on the return trip to Antioch.

Preaching in the coastal areas when they first passed through was never stated or implied, nor was any reason given why they moved on so swiftly. But before they embarked to return to Antioch in Syria, they spoke to the people of Perga. Then, without any discussion about the return voyage, they came to Antioch, and since that church had sent them out for the task just completed, a report was both an obligation and a privilege. Much had been done in offering the gospel to the Gentiles and the responses they had received. It would appear that this effort, which we sometimes call the first journey, had begun a different kind of emphasis. Recall that in each case where it seemed possible, Paul and Barnabas had gone first to the Jewish people in the synagogues, and only after the Jews rejected them had the mission become largely oriented toward the Gentiles. That was to uncover another huge mountain, a crisis for the total church.

[1] Rackham, 221.
[2] W.M. Ramsey, *The Church in the Roman Empire* (London: Hodder and Stoughton, 1893), 31ff. and 376-382.

Chapter 11

The Basic Question: Is Salvation by Grace?

Just as had occurred in the synagogues in Antioch and Iconium, the admission of Gentiles into the church created a monstrous mountain at home. The circumcision party (Pharisaic), a segment of the early church, especially in Jerusalem, seems to have never sensed that the new movement was anything more than another sect of Judaism. Perhaps they thought it was the one true sect, but their major fear seems to have been that the control of the movement was slipping away from the orthodox view. Therefore, some of them came to Antioch in Syria, where the great advances had already taken place and numerous non-Jews had become a part of the fellowship. The Jewish representatives, in a sense, attempted to negate the salvation of the Gentiles by saying that it was necessary for the new converts to become Jews (i.e. be circumcised according to the custom of Moses). or else their salvation was not valid. As one might expect, those forward-looking disciples, led by Barnabas and Paul, waged a strong debate. Luke, as is characteristic of him, put it mildly by saying that they had "no small dissension," Which really means that all gloves were off. To this point in the narrative, these people had not been identified with the Judaizers, but they were the nucleus of that segment of the church. The direction they wanted the church to go was to continue in a salvation characterized by doing the things of the law, which Paul opposed. It is not necessary to assume that these people were evil and internal troublemakers. They were serious and committed conservatives who were absolutely convinced that the basic tenets of the movement must not violate Jewish law, customs and observance. Such religious convictions are difficult to examine and, sometimes, almost impossible to overcome. In effect, what they were saying was that the work of Paul and Barnabas, of Philip and Peter, was void or incomplete. Religious debates have never been simple and easy to decide, probably because they always contain so much emotion. Each party comes with strong and often dogmatic convictions which can never be easily laid aside.

The Antioch church, whose decision to go to the Gentiles had been challenged, decided to get the position of the church at Jerusalem under the leadership of the original apostles, since it could not be decided at Antioch. So Paul and Barnabas and others from the church in Antioch made the trek to Jerusalem. (It cannot be determined whether the trip was made as a body or even whether that party included those who had brought up the issue.) It was a crisis of first magnitude, and should the decision have gone with the position of the Judaizers, the Gentile missions would have either stopped completely or required proselyte conversions as well as the belief that Jesus was the Messiah, or there would have been a division into two competing churches, Jewish and Gentile. It is nearly impossible to conceive that Paul and Barnabas and the entire church at Antioch could have agreed to the demands of circumcision and obedience to the Law of Moses as essentials for the salvation of people among whom they had already seen the evidence of the Holy Spirit. While the opinion of the leaders of the Jerusalem church was sought, there is not a hint of willingness to compromise a fundamental conviction. Requiring obedience to Jewish law would alter the doctrine regarding how salvation occurs. Keep in mind that these were not anti-Christian people. They were dedicated, committed followers with strong Pharisaic backgrounds who were convinced that they knew that they had the only proper answer. While those who had first gone to Antioch are reported to have only said that it was necessary for the new converts to undergo circumcision, the discussion at Jerusalem included that "they be ordered to keep the Law of Moses."

After a rather contentious debate, Peter took the lead role, and since he had previously been successful with the same problem, he compared the hearing at Jerusalem with his experience with Cornelius. He used the same tactic in this discussion, that of the leadership of the Holy Spirit. His "punch line" was that God had given the Holy Spirit to the Gentiles just as he had to the community in Jerusalem. Since God had made no distinction, the position of these Judaizers was labeled as "putting God to the test." An interesting passage, which has already been alluded to, is that Peter said, "On the contrary, we believe that *we* will be saved through the grace of the Lord Jesus, just as *they* will." He did not say, "They will be saved just as we are," but just the opposite. To paraphrase it a little differently, Peter said, "Those Gentiles received salvation by faith, and we Jews will be saved in the same way."

Another issue needs to be examined. The Jews believed that the law was the exact word of God. If that were true, to allow the claims of those in the new movement was to say that God had changed or contradicted his word. That is always the difficulty of claiming that the actual words written by men, even under the inspiration of the Holy Spirit, are the exact dictated words of God, for if that is true, there can be *no* deviation or change in any of them.

Acts 15:12-21

Barnabas and Paul were given the opportunity to describe the fantastic events that had occurred on the journey and the successes they had experienced. When they finished, the leading figure in the Jerusalem church, James, the brother of Jesus, made a proposal. James apparently had not been a believer before the resurrection, so it is interesting that he already had such a dominating influence. His proposal was what he had personally concluded, but then the entire church ratified it. Nothing is pointedly said about the argument that was threatening to ruin the church, but rather, with a side mention that no further burden should be laid on the Gentiles, it was an effort to find a way that Jewish Christians and Gentile Christians could develop fellowship. So it really did not address the issue except to deal with "no further burden."

Jewish exclusiveness centered around the law, temple worship, and legalistic observances such as the Sabbath and unclean foods. The Hellenistic movement in the church, the approach of Stephen, the unauthorized preaching of Philip, the radical experience of Cornelius (and his people), the success of the church at Antioch, and the recent work done by Barnabas and Paul were all evidences of progress. But progress often brings resistance. In this chapter (Acts 15), an orderly method was used to work out a solution. A report had been given to the whole church (vv.4-5) along with the claims of the Judaizers. Then a discussion in a smaller group, apostles and elders, seems to have taken place, and there was much disagreement. One more time, Paul and Barnabas were given the opportunity to explain what had taken place on the journey. Then James made a proposal that became the basis for a decision. The matter was brought before the entire church (v.22), and a final decision was reached.

The issues were both theological and practical. From a theological position, they were: (1) Is it at all possible for Gentiles to be saved? If the answer should be "yes" then the question would be raised, must they become Jewish proselytes? (2) Although it is not mentioned in the letter that was sent, the answer to the proselyte issue must have been "no." (3) That would ultimately, though not perhaps at the moment, raise the question as to whether Jewish Christians must still follow the law, but that issue was not addressed. The practical matters were: (1) Can Jewish Christians associate with Gentile Christians? If they could, under what conditions? But that would present a new issue: (2) Must there be two churches? If the answer were to be "yes," then the fundamental principle of unity of the organism would be violated. (3) How could this division be avoided and not create a situation where the Gentile Christians were not "second class?" Obviously, if they were second class, the *koinonia* spirit would be destroyed.

Since James' proposal did not deal with the theological matters, we wonder if that issue might have been considered moot because of Peter's statements. One thing is certain: Gentile Christians were not compelled to undergo circumcision. However, the letter did state that those who had caused the problem had no directive or authority from the church at Jerusalem. The decree was approved and was to be distributed by Barnabas and Paul and two official representatives of the Jerusalem church, Judas (called Barsabbas) and Silas. If the letter had been taken only by Paul and Barnabas, there could have been (and likely would have been) the claim that it represented only their answer and not that of the church at Jerusalem. So two witnesses (Jewish law required two) were sent to authenticate it as representing the position of the church and the authority of the apostles.

The letter in Acts 15:23-29

"The brothers, both apostles and elders, to the believers of Gentile origin in Antioch and Syria, greetings. Since we have heard that certain persons who have gone out from us with no instructions from us, have said things to disturb you and have unsettled your minds, we have decided unanimously to choose representatives and send them to you along with our beloved Barnabas and Paul, who have risked their lives for the sake of our Lord Jesus Christ. We have therefore, sent Judas and Silas, who will tell you the same things by word of mouth. For it has seemed good to the Holy Spirit and to us to impose on you no further burden than these essentials: that you should abstain from what has been sacrificed to idols and from blood, and from what is strangled, and from fornication. If you keep yourselves from these, you will do well. Farewell."

With the exception of the phrase, "It has seemed good to the Holy Spirit and to us to impose on you no further burden than these essentials," the content of the letter is entirely in terms of what is necessary for there to be fellowship with Gentiles who have previously lived in territories where these unacceptable things, at least unacceptable to the Jews, were common:

1. To abstain from all things sacrificed to idols. It was the Jewish understanding that such meats had been contaminated, and therefore fellowship would be strained because of idolatry.

2. To abstain from blood. That was another Jewish "taboo," perhaps because they believed that the life was in the blood and therefore would produce the same kind of contamination that would ensue by eating and drinking blood.

3. To abstain from things that had strangled, which would imply that the blood remained in the body and that would bring contamination. These deal with foods that are "kosher."

4. To abstain from fornication. Fornication is much more inclusive than the term "adultery." Adultery involves sexual intercourse between persons who are not married to each other, a violation of the marriage bond. Fornication is a much more inclusive term and involves persons who are not married. The Jewish commandment dealt just with adultery and involved violating the "property" of the husband. It did not deal with the issue of fornication. However, the Jews considered all sexual activity outside of the marriage relationship as forbidden. The Jewish fear must have been that the Gentiles were more lax and lived in a society where fornication and adultery were not unusual.

Acts 15:30-35

Evidently, the church at Antioch had wondered with anxiety what the outcome of the journey would be. It was of critical importance to them, for in one sense they may have believed that their salvation hung on the outcome. Certainly their unity with the Jerusalem community did. It has already been noted that all of the earliest followers were sincere followers of Judaism. At least since the time of Ezra, Judaism had demanded a separation from the Gentile world both religiously and culturally. Much of the non-Jewish world knew of the law and its high moral standards. It also knew there were certain "taboos" that, while they may not have been a problem for the Gentiles, did impose some restraints on good Jews. It is most likely that there were many conservative, rigid Jews, but there were also those who attempted to bridge the Jew-Gentile gap. This was true in Judaism, and it carried over into the Christian community. However, the expansive vision of some members of the Christian community agitated the exclusiveness which prompted the conference recorded in Acts 15. Since the time of the captivity, many Jews had opposed any worship of idols/images. One of the important teachings that came out of the captivity was that laxness in regard to idolatry had actually produced the fall of the nation. This can be seen in the Ten Commandments and in the voices of the prophets. However, such worship was common in the Gentile world. The Jews had certain restrictions on food, such as pork. Why those restrictions developed among the Jews and were incorporated into their worship system is difficult to ascertain. It may well be that because they were wandering as a group of desert nomads, it was difficult to prepare pork, and it often caused digestive disturbances. A logical conclusion, according to their theology, would have been that it was sinful to eat those meats. Other meats were obnoxious to consider, such as that of vultures or reptilian species. Whatever may have been the origin of those taboos, they did produce cultural stress.

In opposing idolatry, it also came to be the position that any meat offered to an idol inherently implied that one was participating in the idol worship. So from a cultural/religious point of view, conflicts were inevitable unless the church remained totally Jewish, including those Gentiles who were Jewish proselytes. Although it may appear that the issue was solved at the conference, the problem continued as a type of salvation in which the worshipper earned his salvation.

Chapter 12

Further Expansion to the Gentiles

❖

Acts 15:36-41

Armed with the decision and the approval of the apostles, Paul and Barnabas decided to re-visit the converts in what we know as Asia Minor. Differences in personalities often produce conflicts, but they can also be seen as evidence of what will later be called diverse "gifts of the Spirit." Barnabas was known as a noble person of consolation, but a conflict arose between him and Paul as they prepared to return to the churches. It may have involved more than just personality differences. Perhaps Barnabas knew or understood more of the reasons why John Mark had left the party and was more sympathetic, but by his very nature he seems to have been willing to offer second chances. He had certainly interceded for Paul when he first came to the church at Jerusalem. If that spirit is coupled with the knowledge that Mark was his nephew, it is easy to see why he wanted to give him another opportunity. Paul, who must have told this story to Luke, saw Mark as a deserter and, therefore, unreliable. The position taken in this work is that on the earlier journey Mark may have had difficulty when he saw the pace of the advancement to the Gentiles. We may never know the bitter feelings that may have been voiced, but it is evident that Paul was not comfortable with taking Mark along this time. That did not necessarily have anything to do with forgiveness; it had to do with the estimate of both Paul and Barnabas regarding Mark's dependability. This may be another of those times when Paul could look back and come to the conclusion that he penned in Romans 8:28 — when properly translated (see page 23). Paul and Barnabas parted company, and Barnabas took Mark and went to Cyprus. Paul chose Silas and returned to the areas he had first visited. It did make two for missionary efforts, and therefore an amplification of the work. This is also evidence of what Leslie Weatherhead called the "Circumstantial Will of God."[1] Another internal barrier, or mountain, had been overcome, and this time it dealt with a divisive personal issue. This is not intended to imply that God caused the break-up, but to show that in spite of it he was able to use both Barnabas and Paul, and also Mark. Often, especially with beginning servants, time is needed for both growth and development. What a shame it would have been if the Christian mission had completely lost this servant who later penned our first gospel, the Gospel of Mark.

Acts 16:1-5

It was fitting that the decision from the apostles should be delivered in Antioch, in Syria, and in Cilicia, for it concerned them all. It would be interesting if we knew the "tug of war" that went on in the mind of Paul in regard to the circumcision of Timothy. It should be apparent that such was not necessary for Timothy's salvation for he had already earned the respect of the Christian communities in Lystra and Iconium. However, Paul was about to go into other areas and would probably use the same pattern of going first to the synagogues. If Timothy were to go along and be accepted in those synagogues, he would, by necessity, have had to be circumcised, thus becoming a proselyte. But this was a matter of expediency, for as Paul would explain later, "neither circumcision nor un-circumcision" would amount to anything. This did not in any way compromise what had been gained in Jerusalem. From town to town, the church was strengthened, and it grew. The narrative has now reached the completion point of Paul's plan to inform the people about the decision from the church in Jerusalem. This did not mean that he would not share that letter with new Gentile converts. Since it was a milestone in the progress of the church, he would have used it wherever it was appropriate.

Acts 16:6-10

These verses are a transition to get the party to where the mission to Macedonia would begin. In a rapid telling of what may have taken place in Antioch of Pisidia and other towns, the party moved through Asia toward the seaport of Troas. Apparently there was some discussion concerning the desire to preach in other areas, but they were convinced that the Spirit was not leading them to establish a mission in Asia or to some of the northern areas, Bithynia in particular, at this time. (Notice that once the leadership is called the "holy Spirit" and once it is called "the Spirit of Jesus.") Both of those were Roman provinces in what is now called Turkey. Churches developed later in Asia (cf. Colossae, Laodicea,

Ephesus, Thyatira, Pergamum, and some other towns), but on this trip there was no effort made in Asia. It is rather astonishing how quickly Luke narrated the Troas mission and indicated that he became a member of the party. (cf. see the "we" sections) Since dreams and visions often have their sources in prior events, it may well be that Luke, possibly Macedonian himself, was converted and pled for Paul to undertake a mission to his home area.

It would be helpful if we were to know what circumstances Paul met when he returned to the Galatian area. At some point he must have discovered what he would have considered a subversive effort on the part of the Judaizers, and his anger became so strong that he wrote a scathing letter to his converts showing how the Judaizers had corrupted the message. This was the most significant mountain the new movement had confronted, and it threatened to destroy the unity of the body of Christ. Because of the decision of the Conference (recorded in Acts 15), the Galatian letter, and Paul's intense reaction, it is fitting to turn aside and discuss Paul's vigorous defense of his gospel as it is seen in the book of Galatians. For the purposes of this work, this culminates the remarkable transformation of the Christian gospel from an exclusive legalistic religion to a gospel of grace/faith.

[1]Leslie Weatherhead, *The Will of God* (Nashville: The Abingdon Press, 1972), 27ff.

Chapter 13

The Controversy Carried to Galatia

There is little or no doubt about the authorship of the book of Galatians, but there is some uncertainty as to when it was written. It may be the first of many letters that Paul wrote, and it deals with what he believed was the most significant issue facing the church at the time. Numerous scholars have argued for different dates, but most of them place it between 49 and 51 C.E. The position taken here is based on conjecture regarding what may have happened after certain people came down from Jerusalem to Antioch to straighten out the "heresy" that allowed Gentiles to become a part of the church without first becoming Jewish proselytes. The church at Antioch chose to submit the issue to the apostles and the church at Jerusalem. At this particular time in the life of the church, those apostles were considered the ones most likely to have the correct answer, since they had been closest to Jesus. (The following conjecture is that of the author.)

Perhaps some of the group did not go to the conference but went instead to the churches in Galatia for the distinct purpose of correcting the error that the church at Antioch and Paul and Barnabas had made. What they succeeded in doing, however, was confusing the believers so that when Paul and Silas came through after the conference and read the conference's letter to them, they found utter confusion and many damaging doubts. Even after trying to calm the believers during the rather quick visit, Paul found it necessary to write a more thought-out position and present it in this letter. This conjecture will also accept that the visit to Jerusalem, to which Paul referred in the second chapter of Galatians, was the one made for the conference and discussed in Acts 15. Something made Paul absolutely furious, for when one reads Galatians carefully, especially in the original, it is white hot with anger. Since the decision at the conference went his way, what could make him this furious? Had there been some "behind the back" method that had been used without waiting for the decision from the conference? Remember that during the discussion and in the letter to the Gentile churches, it was said that the group that went to Antioch did so without authorization from Jerusalem. Galatians had to be written after the journey Paul and Barnabas had made, because in the visit to which Paul refers, he took Titus, who was a Gentile and must have been well known to the Galatians. (Titus was probably from the Galatian area.) This would suggest that when Paul and Silas came through the area, they found discouragement, confusion, and the communities in disarray, perhaps because some of the Judaizers had acted before the conference decision and distorted the message, causing grave doubts about Paul's apostleship. The main group, whomever it was composed of, had made the journey to Jerusalem in good faith, believing that they were all seriously attempting to get the opinion of the apostles. For some of them to have gone to Galatia without waiting for the decision would have been an unethical act and would have certainly destroyed the fellowship of the people involved. So after passing through the area and seeing the confusion and despair that the Judaizers had created, Paul saw the need for a carefully thought-out defense of his position. That defense could have been written from Troas, Philippi, or even Corinth in late 49 or 51 C.E. Two other possibilities have been suggested. 1) Galatians could have been written before the conference, but if this were the case, it would create a problem relative to the second chapter of Galatians; or 2) Paul could have written the letter immediately after his return from the Jerusalem Conference and before he set out with Silas to visit Galatia. The second possibility would require some unknown source of information concerning what the Judaizers had done, which would not be impossible because the Christians at Antioch may have known what the Judaizers planned to do. But it would also make one ask why Paul thought a letter would be better than an immediate visit to clear up the situation. Readers will have to draw their own conclusions, because we have no information regarding what took place. One should not be shocked that dogmatic Christian men, who knew that they had the correct answer, would have taken it upon themselves to correct this terribly wrong theological situation without any approval or direction — something that has happened many, many times in religious and Christian history.

Galatians 1:1-10

There are two major issues in this letter. One has to do with the validity of Paul's apostleship. That apostleship was unique — even Paul admits as much — so those who were trying to discredit him and his teaching could argue that he was not a valid apostle. The second, which to Paul was even more important, is the nature of Christian salvation. As Paul saw the issue, it really posed two different kinds of gospel. The one he had proclaimed comes by faith only, and therefore is a gift from God which comes only through his grace. It is completely undeserved and unearned by works. In making his argument, Paul showed that he had some major doubts about the genuineness of the motives of the Judaizers. One must always be aware in these letters that we have only one side of the debate and must reconstruct what we can of the other side.

Paul's defense of his apostleship was rather simple and required only a bold claim. He did not get his authority from any human source or commission, which would have been through the apostles at Jerusalem. His claim came directly from God through the risen Lord. He must have felt that there was no other argument to be made, and that what he claimed must be accepted by the Galatians or their original introduction to the message — and to Paul's authority — had to be rejected.

Paul expressed great astonishment that anyone who had experienced what the Galatians had could so easily be confused. (The language seems to say that he was "bug-eyed.") He indicated that they were being tempted to turn away from the grace of Christ to another gospel of a completely different kind. The term used to express "another" is *heteros*, which means another of a different kind, such as our term "hetero-sexual," and he immediately strengthened it by saying that it was not another of the same kind, using the word *allo*. That would mean that some were trying to pervert the very nature of the good news and were confusing the believers. Even though Paul expressed astonishment, it is easy to see how relatively new converts (novices) could be led astray by people who were from Jerusalem and could probably claim to have been closer to the Lord. Incidentally, if the theory concerning the position John Mark was supposed to have filled on that first journey is correct, one can also see why Paul was so disturbed when Mark reneged on his commitment. (See the above discussion on Acts 14:36ff.) So Paul made a harsh statement (1:8) that if he himself came back and changed the message, or even such an authority as an angel from heaven made the change, that one should be *anathema*, meaning accursed or "damned!" The statement is what is called a "third class conditional statement" and means "if we or anyone else makes such a different claim, and for purposes of this argument we may or may not, but if that happens the person is to be cut off, or 'damned'." This was immediately repeated using the following "first class conditional sentence:" "If anyone preaches contrary to what you have received, and they have done that, they are to be damned." It was not good enough to say it once. Paul reinforced it by repeating the same curse with another Greek linguistic tool. Evidently, those who had tried to discredit his teaching had suggested that he was watering down the demands of the gospel to please men and make it easier. It is almost impossible to express those ideas in English strongly enough. He stated that he could not be doing so because it would run counter to his being a servant of Christ.

Galatians 1:11-124

There has been much debate regarding to which visit to Jerusalem the one recorded in Galatians 2 corresponds. Some have sensed that in Acts there are actually three visits, one coming shortly after Paul's conversion, one coming when he and Barnabas took the offering from Antioch to Jerusalem, and one which is most often called the Jerusalem Conference. In this letter, Paul mentions only two visits, and therefore some have proposed that the Galatians 2 passage refers to the visit when he and Barnabas took the offering. However, in the passage about the "offering visit," there is no mention of any conference with the apostles or any theological disturbance. In Galatians, Paul referred to visits to show that he did not get his authority from the apostles, but from God. Therefore, there would have been no need to mention the famine visit, since it had nothing to do with the proclamation of the gospel to the Gentiles and there was probably no contact with the apostles. The first visit to Jerusalem would then be the one mentioned in Galatians 1:18-19, which would correspond to the visit when Paul was first brought to the Jerusalem church and Barnabas vouched for him. The second visit, in which there was contact with the disciples, would be recorded in Acts 15 and would correspond to Paul's account in Galatians 2. That he took Titus with him on that visit would require that it would have occurred after the journey he and Barnabas had made into the Galatian territory. The "false believers" would be those who were teaching that there was no salvation without circumcision and adherence to the Mosaic law. Paul nearly always believed that he was doing something or going somewhere under the leadership of the Spirit, so going to Jerusalem under "revelation" would certainly be how he would describe that visit. One can sense that while Paul did not reject the leadership role of the apostles, he was not dependent on their approval.

Earlier, there was a suggestion that the church could have been split by this controversy. The tone of Paul's account would at least hint at the idea that if the decision had gone in favor of the Judaizers, he would still have continued to preach the same message to the Gentiles. While in Acts, Peter refers to the idea that he was charged to go to the Gentiles (Cornelius), the thrust of Paul's argument was that Peter (Aramaic — "Cephas") was the one to lead the ministry to the Jews, while he, Paul, was primarily responsible for the ministry among the Gentiles. This did not mean that the two areas of work were in conflict; it simply meant that the primary responsibilities were as Paul described them in Galatians, and the "pillars" of the Jerusalem Church agreed with the position Paul had taken. In Galatians, there is no mention of the letter from the conference. That letter was primarily sent to Antioch, but it is probable that Paul and Silas read it to the Gentile churches as they passed through. The only request in this passage is to "remember the poor," which those in Antioch had already done and would continue to do.

Galatians 2:11-21

No passage demonstrates more clearly the strength of Paul's conviction about a right relationship with God being established by faith alone. We have no record of this confrontation in Acts, but it must have posed another problem. In many ways, Peter seems at times to have been wishy-washy. He had been called a stone in the building of the church (Matthew 16:18) and had made a strong argument at the conference, but he is shown here not to have much strength to stand against the Judaizers. To accept Cornelius or the people at Antioch when there was no one else around to counter that stand was relatively easy. But Peter's basic conviction must have been that which he had learned in the Cornelius encounter, yet when the strong "ultra-conservative" Jews were around, he did not have the "guts" to stand alone. But he was not the only one. The text, literally translated, says that Barnabas was "hypocrited away" with the others. There is no English verb to make that translation. But the statement is stronger than "he was led away."

At least in this confrontation, Paul believed that the inconsistency was so serious that it would have led to a "different gospel of another kind." The argument seems to have been something like this: Peter had been willing to eat with Gentiles, fellowship with them, and do other things that Jewish law forbade, at least when no one was around to oppose that position. (Who has not found himself/herself alone in talking a stand in an unpopular situation and knowing the difficulty in talking such a stand?) We need to see Peter's weakness not in judgment, but in the light of our own inability to always be consistent. So when the Judaizers showed up, Peter violated the position he had learned in the Cornelius experience. Someone has said, "It is only about a foot between my head and my heart, but sometimes it is a lifetime journey." We are all learners, St. Paul included, and we sometimes find ourselves ashamed of our inconsistencies. Learning is really hard.

Many scholars believe that the quotation marks, which represent Paul's reprimand to Peter, should be placed at the end of the chapter instead of at verse 14. There were no quotation marks in the original; they were placed there by the editors/translators. If the entire passage explains Paul's statement to Peter, it makes good sense that all those in the wayward group were Jewish Christians and could not be classified as "Gentile sinners." However, Paul argued, everyone knows that justification comes by faith in Jesus and is not something one earns by keeping the law or doing good deeds. The term "justification" means "to put right in relationship" (in this case with God), and while it was a legal term, its primary emphasis here was to remove the barrier separating humans from God, which can only be done by the grace of God and acceptance of the gift through faith. In Paul's writings, faith means unreserved commitment. So if one has claimed to have been put in right relationship with God and then turns back to a legalistic concept of earning that relationship by keeping the law, he/she is building again the kind of religion in which one earns his/her relationship by works and it cannot be by grace. Either the position stated at the Jerusalem Conference that "we are saved just like they (Gentiles) are" is to be maintained, or we renege on our commitment and become transgressors.

Paul's concept that he had died to the law and come alive in Christ, "that I might live to God," demanded that the old rebellious ego must be put to death and a new life begun as Christ lives in us. But Paul did not consider this to be easy, nor was it something that was done one time with no later repercussions. In fact, he indicated that one of the things that leads to individual progress and growth was involvement in a continual battle with the old self. This seems to mean that a decision to allow Christ to be Lord constantly runs into inner opposition; apparently one never dies to self completely. It was in this sense that Paul wrote, "I have been crucified with Christ and it is not I that live, but Christ lives in me" (not literally or physically, but in the sense that the old ego-controlled life is to end). This was the essence of his gospel. Recall that in a practical way he later wrote in Corinthians 15:31, "I die daily." But anything less than that or contrary to that, by adding other requirements, is a perversion of the concept of grace — and actually nullifies grace. As Paul saw it, if there was any other way to Christian salvation than through faith commitment, the entire life of Jesus, and most surely his death, was completely useless.

Chapter 14

Retrogression Denies Abraham's Experience

Galatians 3:1-14

The translation "O Foolish Galatians" does not represent exactly what Paul meant, for he would not have intentionally insulted people. The phrase appears to mean something like, "O you Galatians who have been hood-winked." The entire thrust of the paragraph implies that someone has pulled the wool over their eyes. It is not that they are stupid, but that they have been deceived, for the completion of the thought states that someone (later identified as the Judaizers) put the evil eye on them, or hexed them. Paul had just finished saying that any turn to this other gospel made the crucifixion of Jesus a meaningless thing. Now that they have heard the message of the death and resurrection of Jesus, how could any of them who have received the Spirit in that glorious breath of fresh air of forgiveness and blessing ever back-track on that experience? The major question was not whether they had received the Spirit, but how did it come about, and the answer should be simple. If they had begun their new life in the Spirit, surely, they should know that turning to some other way to gain God's favor would be ridiculous. They had not been brought to this new experience by obeying the law, so the question would be, if they initially received the Spirit and God's working among them by believing (which for Paul always meant "committing one's self to") what they were taught by Barnabas and Paul, what would make them think that they could gain anything else by accepting the demands of the law? The only thing that could have made them even consider the possibility was if someone claiming insight and having more authority than Paul and Barnabas had been able to deceive them.

Then Paul used a rabbinical argument to prove his point. He found an Old Testament passage stating that Abraham believed God, which allowed him to gain right relationship. One must always remember that for Paul, "to believe" (the root term is *pisteuo*) was to commit oneself without any reservation, so it was not just Abraham's intellectual assent to which he referred, but the commitment of life-changing obedience. The implication was that God had always intended to bring about reconciliation (right relationship) of the Gentiles, and just as it occurred in the life of Abraham because of commitment (faith), it also came about among the Gentiles. The quotation from Habakkuk 2:4 actually stated that regardless of what difficulties one might face, the righteous man will persevere because of faithfulness. When that passage was translated in the Septuagint (which is the Hebrew translated into Greek), the term used was *pistis*, which meant faith commitment. Paul must have used the Septuagint in this case, so his argument was that man lives because of his faith.[1]

According to the argument, to turn to doing works of the law for one's right relationship would put one under the curse referred to in Deuteronomy 27:26 and 28:58ff. An immature faith might easily be sabotaged by one claiming to have the authority of the original apostle group. The consequence would be that any error in observing everything written in the material listed in Deuteronomy would result in being cursed. Obviously, the law was not of faith, but only of deeds. Paul then went on to say that Christ had bought us out from under the curse mentioned above by dying on our behalf. That argument also requires that the one dying must not deserve to die because of any personal disobedience. The reference to Christ removing the curse by hanging on a tree is also a proof text from Deuteronomy 21:23, which concerned itself with instruction about dealing with the body of one who had been convicted of a crime, executed, and his body exposed by hanging on a tree. Only an educated rabbi could construct such an argument, which might not carry the same weight in the twenty-first century. The primary thrust of the argument was that just as the faith of Abraham brought about his right relationship, that same concept brings about the right relationship of all who, like Abraham, share in faith.

Galatians 3:15-18

The illustration Paul used to reinforce his argument was a simple one that still applies in modern law: A will cannot be altered or added to by anyone except the testator, and after it has been written and attested to, it is an inviolable document. (Obviously, there are times in current legal practice when efforts to alter or break a will are successfully made.) The argument was that the covenant of faith occurred some 430 years before the giving of the law, and therefore it still retained its original significance and authority. The little sentence ("Now the promises were made to Abraham and to his offspring; it does not say, and to offsprings as of many, but it says, and to your offspring, that is to one person who is Christ.") does not detract from the argument. The term offspring is from the Septuagint and is singular. But as most commentators sense, Paul has been using a rabbinical exegetical method emphasizing the singular noun as a collective noun. This can be seen in English, since words like sheep, deer, and seed are collective. The use of seeds is possible, although if the term is translated "offspring," the plural would not be used. What Paul was saying was that the covenant with Abraham was made in faith and did not depend on the law, because the law came much later. So there cannot be any case in which the law supplants the covenant of promise — which means that the early covenant is still in effect

> "What Paul has in mind in verse 16 is that, according to the reading of Jewish history, the promises made to Abraham and his offspring (of 'seed' f. Gen. xiii, 15ff; xvii, 7 ff.) were not really fulfilled until the coming of Christ, and this is in line with Scripture, which use the singular 'offspring' and not the plural: the singular therefore, can only refer to Christ. . . . He is not *allegorizing* the scripture as he does in iv: 22ff; he is *spiritualizing* it, looking at it in the light of his gospel."[2]

However, the thrust is still on the validity of "faith" as opposed to deeds of law. It cannot and could not be both ways. Either God's original message to Abraham involved accepting the promise by faith commitment or it was abrogated by the giving of the law, which Paul would not allow.

Galatians 3:19-29

If there were no saving power in the law, which was Paul's main contention in this passage, then there had to be an explanation for why there should be law. In any religion of works (whether keeping commandments or earning merit), the basic problem that arises is that of pride, and pride was one of the early factors in the concept of sin that separated man from God. Paul argued that the law was brought in so that sin could be seen as transgression. The meaning of the term *hamartia* is to miss the mark, even in ignorance, but transgression is an act of disobedience that can only occur if there are proscriptions. While he had already acknowledged the existence of faith in the case of Abraham, Paul still held that with the coming of Jesus, a fresh avenue of acceptance by God was available.

Paul also followed a rabbinical concept that the law was given through the mediation of angels, which was a tradition developed in Deuteronomy 33:2 and

Psalm 68:17. That idea was also referred to in Stephen's sermon in Acts 7:38 and later in Hebrews 2:2, as well as in several non-canonical Jewish works and in Josephus. Apparently, the rabbinic position was that some being or beings had to stand between man and God to bring the law into effect. There are numerous interpretations of this passage, and it is extremely difficult to be certain as to its meaning. One highly plausible meaning, in keeping with the total argument of this section, is that in the giving of the law, Moses (and/or angels) became the mediator(s). But in the promise to Abraham, there was no mediator; God dealt directly. This would imply that there is a unity of God seen in Christ (compare Paul's idea that "God was in Christ"), and no mediator was needed. The purpose of the passage appears to be to show that the function of the law was simply to edify and make people aware of their shortcomings, not to produce salvation. The law was an interpolated bit of information needed only to show the real nature of sin. Paul believed that obedience to the law was never a part of God's intention relating to salvation.

As a result, the scripture (commandments) imprisoned all things under the power of sin, and there was no relief except through faith in Jesus Christ. This did not mean that the law was in any sense antagonistic to the promises of God. Paul used his favorite expression of utter impossibility (*me genoito*) to render the idea absurd.[3]

So what *was* the condition of mankind before Christ came? Salvation even then functioned through faith commitment, but the law served as a pedagogue to lead us to Christ. In Paul's world, a pedagogue was a servant charged with the responsibility of taking the master's children to school. This meant that the law served to bring mankind to the place where they could see the need for Christ and be taught in terms of faith in him. While the Judaizers claimed that circumcision and obedience to the law were a part of salvation, Paul insisted that only faith mattered. There could no longer be any distinction between Jew and Greek; even the distinctions between slaves and owners were no longer valid. (One should remember that in the letter to Philemon, Paul admonished the slave owner to treat the slave, Onesimus, who had become a Christian, as a brother. Paul does not seem to have crusaded against the slavery of his day, but he did "cut off the legs" on which it stands.) Neither can there be any distinction between males and females. *There are no second-class citizens in the kingdom of God, for all are one in Christ.* Regardless of what the Judaizers may have said, the Gentiles (Galatians) were Abraham's offspring because of the promise. Paul understood that this new message was radical and life-altering, but it was not an armed revolution. Its basic ideas were revolutionary, but it was a moral revolution. It should be obvious that if Paul or any other first-century leader had taken a position against the slavery of the Roman Empire, the movement would likely have been crushed. (Even an aggressive campaign against the subordination of women would have produced the same result, but what Paul did was to sow the seeds that would later produce freedom for everyone.) So in all cases, Paul simply proclaimed a principle out of which future generations would understand that making second-class citizens of anyone would be contrary to the unity of the body and to the liberation theme of the gospel as Jesus taught it. Regardless of those passages which may deal with special circumstances in regard to women, Paul saw that the gospel would ultimately revolutionize any thought about domination or superiority, whether it be the abolition of slavery, racial inequality, the equality of women and children, or the liberation of the powerless or oppressed. Church history shows that there have always been those who refused to see this theme of equality, and some still do.

Galatians 4:1-11

The argument in Chapter 3 had shown that the law was inferior to faith. In Hebrew, Greek, and Roman law, a boy was in an inferior (immature) position until he became of age. To some extent, this appears to be true in most cultures until the age that a boy is determined to be a mature male. For the Hebrews, this was about the time of puberty, around twelve. The Bar Mitzvah decreed that the boy had become a man. In Greek and Roman societies, boys were a little older before they became of age. That would make no difference here, since 'Paul's argument illustrated that the law was like a childhood experience until the time the father had set. Paul used a term which is translated "the elemental spirits of the world" to describe the law and other possible religious ideas or objects, and suggests that to go back to those kinds of beliefs would be to go back to childhood experiences. But when the father decreed that the child was mature (whether he be Hebrew, Greek, or Roman), the boy moved into the mature realm, which Paul parallels with the faith experience. The phrase "when the fullness of time had come" must parallel the time when the boy is considered mature. There may have been many things interpreters have seen as belonging to that "fullness of time," such as law and order, travel, postal services, or the almost universal usage of Koine' Greek. One might even consider the decay of the various religions and the almost universal longing for something else as fitting here. It is also possible that the meaning of "the fullness of time" had to do with the maturing of the human family unto the point that they could understand Christ. Whether Paul had any or all of those things in mind or not, he certainly meant to convey that with the coming of Jesus and the experience of faith, an avenue had been opened and the Galatians had partaken of it, but only through faith. He certainly feared that they were tempted to return to their old ways, or to turn to the Jewish law; if they did, his work among them had been in vain. One may argue that once the Christian experience has become real for an individual, it will not be revoked. This is certainly true from the point of view of God's gift of grace. Whatever Paul believed about what is called "the security of the believer," he appears in these passages to relate it to an individual's choice. To renounce his/her faith and return to the old ways would have created a situation in which everything that he/she had experienced would have been for nothing. To Paul, such a decision would be a ridiculous choice, but it was a real problem for him, not just an academic exercise. Whatever one may hold concerning that potential renunciation and return to the old or other concepts, the only thing that could possibly bring it about would be the choice of the individual to repudiate what he/she had professed. In the modern world, there have been those who have renounced their faith in Christ and turned to other beliefs. It must be said that such a situation would not be just the committing of a sin, but a complete renunciation of one's loyalty to Christ as Lord. It should also be noted that such a situation is not due to God withdrawing his grace, but to man's renunciation caused by, some might say, a lack of a solid grounding. But for Paul, there is nothing to turn to except some inferior environment.

[1] John A. Allan, *The Epistle to the Galatians* (London: SCM Press, 1957), 61,62.
[2] James Moffatt, *The Epistle of Paul to the Galatians* (New York and London: Harper and Brothers, 1934), 105.
[3] J.Raymond Stamm, *Interpreter's Bible*, vol. 10 (New York-Nashville: Abingdon Press, 1953), 514-516.

Chapter 15

An Appeal for Personal Loyalty

Galatians 4:12-20

In this section, Paul appealed to the Galatians out of reference to the past and their concern for him — a completely different point of view. Any devotion based on emotional response is fickle, but still it was strong enough that Paul used it to attempt to persuade them not to abandon the gospel that he had proclaimed. He had, for all practical purposes, become, as they were, a Gentile! He had come to them and offered himself and the gospel out of an infirmity. We have no way of determining exactly what that physical condition was. We assume, from what Luke says, that there was no mission in Perga when the party first came into the area. We also know that one of the plagues in the area was malaria. If the group came to Perga at the wrong time, they might have run into malaria and decided to move to a higher altitude in the mountainous area north of Perga. If that were the case, terrific headaches and chills might have bothered some of the party, but one cannot help but wonder why that would bring forth the statement that Paul was not scorned or rejected. It has been suggested that the idea of not being scorned meant that they did not reject him by spitting on him. Paul believed that the mission had been welcomed with the best of good will, and he wonders why that good will should change? Others have taken the reference concerning the willingness of the Galatians to tear out their own eyes and the later reference that Paul wrote the signature passage in large letters and with his own hand (6:11) to indicate that he had some kind of residual problem with his vision, perhaps stemming from the blinding light during his conversion experience on the road to Damascus, which could have left him with a squinting, eye-watering problem. Maybe that was his "thorn in the flesh," and it could well have created a continuing issue. It has also been suggested that his rejection by his family, particularly his wife, because of his decision to become a believer could have been what bothered him, but even if that were true it should not have been an observable physical difficulty. Whatever the issue, the good will should still count for something and should continue.

The entire idea seems to be that Paul was trying to appeal to their former friendship and devoted caring to show that the Judaizers were using the Galatians and were trying to lure them into the bondage of Judaism with circumcision and obedience to the law and its requirements. The anguish with which he was dealing was characterized by alluding to the pain of childbirth and by pointing out how his beloved children were being used and confused. Anyone who has ever tried to solve an issue by writing a letter knows how difficult it may be to get the argument across when tone of voice or change of expression are not available.

Galatians 4:21-31

At this point, Paul turned to allegorizing a passage in the Old Testament record. The argument may seem strange to modern ears, but it was common among the rabbinical schools to use several methods of interpretation.

> 1. The method of simple, literary studies was called *Peshat*. It was the first but clearly not the only or best method for finding the meaning of scripture.
>
> 2. The second method was to search for the implied or suggested meaning. It was called *Remaz*.
>
> 3. The third method was called *Derush*, and the meaning was deduced by investigation.
>
> 4. The fourth method was the allegorical, and it was called *Sod*. It was a common usage among the rabbis and was valued as much as the other methods.

The first letters of these four (PRDS) are the consonants of the word "Paradise." When a man succeeded in penetrating these four different meanings, he reached the joy of Paradise.

> "It is to be noted that the summit of all the meanings was the allegorical meaning. It therefore, often happened that the rabbis would take a simple bit of historical narrative from the Old Testament and read into

it inner meanings which often appear to us fantastic, which were very convincing to the people of their day. Paul was a trained rabbi; and that is what he is doing here. He takes the story involving Abraham, Sarah, Hagar, Ishmael, and Isaac (Genesis 16-18), which in the Old Testament is a straightforward narrative and he allegorizes it to illustrate his point."[1]

Anyone who has read the story in the Old Testament is aware that Abraham and Sarah were old and had no children. Abraham attempted to adopt his old servant, Eliezer, to satisfy the condition of the promise, but that appeared to be unacceptable, so the promise was still unfulfilled. Then Sarah decided to help God by giving the slave girl, Hagar, to Abraham to see if a child could be born. In that time, it would have been considered a normal and legal event, and certainly not immoral. When Ishmael was born, Abraham's firstborn according to the text, Abraham was 86 years old (Genesis 16:16). Ishmael's birth, according to Paul, was a completely physical event and had nothing to do with the promise. Sometime later, the unexpected happened; Isaac, the child of promise, was born to Sarah when Abraham was 100 years old (Genesis 21:5). The entire situation created numerous problems from the beginning; the frustrations and conflicts between Hagar and Sarah led to much jealousy and even hatred. Once, when Sarah saw Ishmael either mocking Isaac or playing with him (Ishmael would have been fourteen years older than Isaac), Sarah decided something had to be done. At that point, Abraham allowed Sarah to choose to cast Hagar and Ishmael out, apparently with no concern about what happened to them. Then the Abrahamic line of descent moved through Isaac, and Ishmael became the ancestor of the Ishmaelites. (The Islamic religion argues that Abraham visited and cared for Ishmael and so claims that lineage from Abraham.) Literally, the Jewish people were descendants of Abraham through the promise (Isaac), and the outcast ones were the descendants of slavery.

In typical rabbinic fashion, Paul set up an allegory. In an allegory, one may use any identification he/she deems appropriate to the argument. So Paul set up the allegory to look something like the following:

According to the literal story:

Abraham	Abraham
|	|
Sarah = freedom	Hagar = bondage
|	|
Isaac	Ishmael
|	|
Jewish descendants	Arabian descendants (slavery)

According to the allegory:

Abraham	Abraham
|	|
Sarah = Freedom	Hagar = Bondage
||	||
Isaac	Ishmael
|	|
the New Jerusalem	Mount Sinai & legal bondage
|	|
Christian freedom through faith	Jews in legal bondage

CONCLUSION: The Jews are Hagar's seed through legal bondage. Christians are Abraham's true seed through Sarah (which equals freedom). So Christians are the offspring of the promise and free from legalism.

When Paul began this allegory, he stated that Sarah and Hagar were two mountains. This allowed him to identify Sarah as the free woman and the mountain of the New Jerusalem, while Hagar, the slave girl, was identified with Mount Sinai, which represented the Mosaic law. In this way, Paul could identify the Christian movement, which was free from the law, as the true offspring of Abraham.

Whatever the modern student thinks of the allegorical method, Paul used it to fortify his argument that faith frees one from legal bondage. In true rabbinical fashion, it clinched the argument for him. Could this imply that Christian followers are the true Israel (cf. Romans 10, 11).

Galatians 5:1-6

The argument continued, however, by stating that to follow the position the Judaizers were taking nullified the meaning of Christ. Insisting upon the act of circumcision (physical circumcision, which bound one to the law) as part of the means to salvation destroyed the meaning and significance of grace, and actually bound the new movement to the Jewish religion as just another sect. Paul plainly stated that neither circumcision nor un-circumcision availed anything. He argued that to accept the "other gospel of a different kind," which the Judaizers were preaching, would be to turn away from the concept of grace. While this may sound harsh to modern ears, Paul claimed that acceptance of the law as having any redeeming significance would be to cut one's self off from the significance and meaning of Christ. It should be obvious that if "grace" means undeserved favor, there can be no action to earn it, or it would not be grace. They are mutually exclusive.

Galatians 5:7-12

"You were running well; who prevented you from obeying the truth?" was somewhat of a rhetorical question. Paul knew full well who had distorted the thinking of the Galatians. He seemed confident that when they heard his argument and thought about it, they would reject the position of the Judaizers. One needs to remember that these Judaizers were operating on their own, without any authority from the Jerusalem church, for the position of the Judaizers was not the position taken at the conference. It may be hard to see why the sentence "a little yeast leavens the whole batch of dough" has any significance unless Paul was trying to warn them that to take a little bit of the Judaizers' argument would contaminate the entire concept of grace. Neither can we know all of the insinuations that those opponents had made about Paul, but evidently something had been said to the effect that he was still a practicing Jew and actually followed the same position that they, the Judaizers, did. However, the fact that he was being demeaned (persecuted) showed that he was certainly not in the same camp with them. The statement, "I wish that those who unsettle you would castrate themselves," is harsh. It almost seems as if he was saying that if circumcision were of any value for salvation, cutting off the entire organ would be of more value.

---

[1]William Barclay, *The Letters to the Galatians and Ephesians*, revised edition (Philadelphia: Westminster Press, 1976), 41

Chapter 16

Freedom and Moral Responsibility

Galatians 5:13-15

The fundamentals of the solution Paul offered in the letter were now complete. From this point on, he dealt with personal relationships and behavior. It might be said that a gospel that deals totally with faith cannot provide the proper incentive for ethical behavior. Even though Paul had been thinking about circumcision, food laws, and festival days, he was aware that, especially in a society where moral laxness had been the norm, it now became necessary to challenge the Galatians to a higher standard. It was particularly important for them to know that the teachings about freedom from the ritualistic aspects of the law did not free them from personal responsibility for proper behavior. It has been suggested that verse 13 should be translated, "Do not convert your freedom into an opportunity for indulgence of the flesh," and the lower nature as contrasted with the spiritual.[1] The danger that men would abuse the freedom has been noted throughout the centuries, whereas a religion based on works of the law would require a person to live by a certain code of conduct with its penalties. A remedy has often been seen in Puritanic forms of dress, blue laws, etc. (One must recognize that Paul was not a Gnostic and that his distinction between "flesh" and "spirit" did not imply that material substance itself was evil.)

Paul did not see commitment as something that happened one time and had no lasting effects. The basic truth was that the experience of grace was a life-changing one which aligned one with the Lordship of Christ and worked throughout one's life. To counter the danger that one might possibly think that freedom in faith and freedom from the law lessen the obligation of growing in Christlikeness, he stated that the Galatians should in no way use that freedom as a license for self-indulgence. The concept of *agapé* involves a subordination of ego and an awareness that each follower is to be a servant of others. Paul understood what Jesus said when he noted that the whole law was contained in the commandment to love your neighbor as yourself. Anything less would hinder the expression of Christian unity. On occasions when the church has turned one part against another, it has run the risk of destroying its message and being untrue to its calling. In the contrast between a freedom from the law type of salvation and the binding of oneself to the lordship of Christ, a far more stringent ethical demand is evident than could ever be seen in the law. The ethical responsibility entailed in the lordship of Christ leaves no loopholes.

Galatians 5:16-26

The list of things that characterize the desires of the flesh begins with fornication. As has already been discussed, that term is broader than the term adultery. Adultery involved the marriage relationship and the destruction of human commitment and trust. Fornication is a far more inclusive concept involving all sexual intercourse outside of marriage. From what we know of the Gentiles, it would appear that they not only condoned sexuality, but accepted it as natural and encouraged it in some of the temples. With this challenge, Christianity brought in a completely new virtue.[2] In a modern world that has somewhat reverted to the lax attitude of earlier centuries, this teaching may seem "old-fashioned," but it is the expectation of Christian morality.

Several years ago, the United States military used a slogan that has for ages represented what God intended for humans, although the military intended it to suggest that somehow life in the military could make you "all that you could be." The position taken in the Christian ethic is that God intended each person to become everything he or she could be in the noblest sense. There is no idea that man can achieve "everything" without basic trust in God to lead him into Christlikeness in character. The entire argument of Galatians teaches that attainment of God's intention comes through faith alone. The meaning of the term sin (missing the target) seems to include missing out on what God could do. There has been much discussion about how the world is saturated with selfish desire that contaminates everyone and short-circuits God's intent.[3] All of the things Paul lists as "things of the flesh" contaminate and destroy the potential of what a human can become.

On the other side, all of the "fruits of the spirit" are conducive to one maturing into what God would have him/her be, in complete trust and commitment. This should never be taken to suggest that perfection is expected; being an authentic human being is the goal. Even though society continues to wallow in the problems it has created for itself (and the church also has been and is affected by them), the one great fear is that even in organized Christianity there seems to have been a limited effort to emphasize becoming Christ-like in character. If that is the major goal, we often miss the mark.

Paul instructed the Galatians to search for those fruits of the Spirit. Often it is said that the fruit of a Christian is another Christian. This seems to ignore what Paul listed in the letter, for each of the qualities he mentioned are elements in one's character. This would mean that the fruit produced in a Christian, under God's inspiration, is in these Christ-like qualities. Missions are a vitally important and essential byproduct of what develops. They do not represent an external mimicking of Jesus, but an inward growth in the spirit of Christ's character. There has never been a need to pass laws relative to this spiritual growth. Sometimes the world has seen these qualities as weakness, but there is no need for legalistic control over them.

In seeking to be led by the Spirit, one should come to understand that the egocentric nature of striving for recognition, selfish arguments, and envy, even among people in the Body of Christ, are of the flesh. Every honest person will probably have to admit that those qualities must be overcome if there is to be *koinonia* among us. It is noteworthy that Paul should make this kind of appeal for attitude as well as behavior, but the Galatian stability had almost been destroyed by what those he called "false brothers" had done.

Galatians 6:1-10

The closing passage of the letter reflects the teaching of Jesus about what is to happen when a member of the community commits a transgression. It often seems that the natural reaction to discovering that someone has fallen is to "kick them when they are down." But the purpose of community is to recover people when they fall, and who knows when that may happen to another, even ourselves. There is a possibility that the term "detected" may refer to anticipating a possible sin. This is extremely difficult to do, even in the family, but if there is a spirit of humility and love, it may be possible to help avoid the error. Throughout this passage, the emphasis is on recovery, not judgment. The idea extends to helping one another bear burdens, which has to do with developing the spirit of compassion and caring. The term used for bearing each other's burdens is *bare*, and it deals with any trouble, heaviness, or burden. In any community there are times when one or more of the members is carrying a heavy load. Whenever that occurs, the Christian community should not let anyone feel alone. Most have experienced comfort when others share in the true spirit of *agapé*. However, in the last statement Paul used a different word, *phorton*, which means the cargo of a ship, or even a soldier's pack. There are always some things that one must carry for one's self. Paul did not specify what that load might be, but one is reminded of his "thorn in the flesh."

Another warning occurs in the passage concerning self-estimation. A Christian must always walk a tightrope. Each of us must have a positive concept of our abilities and talents, and we should never forget that we are valuable and loved creations of God. On the other side is the danger, especially with those who seem to have more talents, that they think they are more important than they really are. They need to guard against this temptation with intense honesty. Every action, whether thinking too highly of one's self or laboring with an inferior attitude, carries its own consequences. The Christian recognizes this because God has created a moral order, even though at times we seem to ignore it.

Galatians 6:11-18

The authenticity of the letter was vital, so Paul signed it personally. Some have wondered just what "large letters" could mean. The most obvious answer is that Paul could not see well, or some loss of motor skills made it necessary to make large letters. It certainly did not deal with capital letters, for all of the ancient manuscripts were written in "uncials." It demonstrates that Paul used an amanuensis. In this instance it was probably Silas. The final benediction includes a reference to bearing the *stigmata* of Christ. The story Luke told, and the events to which Paul must have been a party to, are not exhaustive, so it may never be known just what those marks were, but they could have been scars suffered when Paul was stoned or during some other event that we have no information about. But the message moved ahead, overcoming mountains, even with the opposition of the Jewish segment of the church. The Judaizing issue was not over, but in the final analysis the gospel progress was unhindered.

---

[1]E.D. Burton, *International Critical Commentary on Galatians* (Edinburgh: T.&T. Clark, 1948), 292, 293.

[2]William Barclay, *The Letters to the Galatians and Ephesians*, revised edition (Philadelphia: Westminster Press, 1976), 46.

[3]Mark Biddle, *Missing the Mark: Sin and its Consequences in Biblical Theology* (Nashville: Abingdon Press, 2005), 51-57.

Chapter 17

A New Vision

This work now returns to the narrative of the book of Acts. We have seen the sequence of events that the mission to the Gentiles caused and the Jewish resistance in a segment of the church at Jerusalem. A decision was made by the Antioch church to reach out into territories that, so far as we know, had never been touched. This vision was more far-reaching than the one that included Cornelius and his family, or even the one to Galatia.

> "Without going farther into the complicated historical and geographical questions involved, we must take notice of the religious purpose of this section. Luke means to bring his heroes to Troas by the direct guidance of the Spirit, so that they are ready for the vision of the young man from Macedonia (across the Aegean Sea) calling for help. What is really happening in this section is that Luke is preparing for the next step, crossing of the water into what we now know as Greece."[1]

This second effort launched from Antioch in Syria must have begun around late 49 or early 50 C.E., and continued for about five years. Nothing is ever said about the conversion of Luke to Christianity. As has been indicated before, the narrative of the book of Acts suddenly, without any explanation, begins to add a member to the party by using the first personal pronoun "we," or "us," Which likely means that the author was now a part of the group. That such should occur in immediate connection with the vision that moved Paul to go to Macedonia prompts some effort to explain it. The best that can be offered is that Luke was converted to Christianity and then proceeded to tell Paul about the needs in Macedonia. As has been strongly hinted before, visions and dreams are often the consequences of previous events that the sub-conscious mind holds. God often seems to use such experiences to create a new understanding. If such a thing happened at Troas, Luke may have been reluctant to indicate that he may have been the inspiration for Paul's decision, so he omitted all reference to himself, even his conversion. Whatever God used to bring about this challenge to Paul, the outcome is an extended mission. (Be reminded that when Barnabas and Paul first discussed this trip, it was to visit the churches they had established on their first journey. This extension moved the mission far beyond that. There can, of course, be other possible explanations for the vision.)

Acts 16:11-15

Samothrace was one of the small Aegean Islands directly between Troas and Neapolis. It is implied that they waited there until daybreak and then sailed on to Neapolis. It would have been difficult to navigate the waters at night. The narrative moves on immediately from Neapolis to Philippi, where a ministry was begun. There is no information concerning how they came to look for a place of prayer on the Sabbath. It is possible that Luke was able to steer them in that direction. Paul had always tried to begin his work among Jewish people in the synagogue, if one were available. When there was no synagogue building, the people in the Diaspora often gathered by a sea or river for their worship. Rackham suggests that on the back of the Gangites a simple enclosure had been built that served as a substitute synagogue for those inclined toward Judaism.[2] There they came upon a woman, Lydia, who had considerable position in the town and ran a profitable business selling purple cloth. She was from the Asian town of Thyatira, which was known for its unusual dye and produced a beautiful purple cloth. Lydia was already a worshipper of God, and she listened with keen interest. She and her household (which may have meant her employees) responded to Paul's message and were baptized. (Some have used this passage to justify infant baptism, but that is probably straining the text a bit.) Luke subtly suggests some strength on Lydia's part when she pressed her invitation for the party to stay at her house. He said, "she prevailed on us."

Acts 16:16-24

How long the ministry lasted before the first major difficulty arose cannot be ascertained. At some point, however, there was a confrontation with a slave girl who is described as having fortune-telling powers. Since she was a slave, those who owned her were using her for their own advantage and were apparently making a sizeable profit from her. Luke indicated that the woman's constant cries that Paul and Silas were proclaiming a way of salvation finally became an irritation to Paul. Believing, as was common in the first century, that some spirit had her under its control, he commanded it to come out. (It was not uncommon for religious teachers or philosophers to offer their claims in the agora.) The owners were infuriated because they had lost their "meal ticket," and they dragged Paul and Silas before the magistrates. The charge was fundamentally a Jewish one, and while there was no evidence that they were advocating customs that were anti-Roman, they were perhaps implying that what was being taught was a *religio illicata*. Judaism was considered a *religio licita*, but they were not allowed to aggressively make proselytes. So if that had been a part of the accusation, it would have dealt with making Jewish proselytes. If they were claiming that what was being taught was a *religio illicita*, therefore, Paul and Silas had no legal rights. To squelch any furor, the magistrates ordered a beating without holding a trial. Paul and Silas were stripped and beaten severely by the Roman lectors. Then, without receiving any care for their wounds, they were thrown into prison and fastened securely in stocks. (Some have suggested that this prison was carved out of a rock wall, and the jailer's home was above it.) According to the narrative, the actual reason for their anger was the economic loss.

Acts 16:25-34

Luke tells us that at midnight an earthquake shook the entire place, the stocks were apparently loosened from the wall, and the doors of the prison were shaken off their pivots. The jailer had been given harsh orders that the prisoners should be kept secure, and when this event occurred he must have known that his life would be in danger if the prisoners escaped. (One should remember that earlier in Acts, when Peter escaped from prison, Herod had the guards executed, a practice that was not unusual.) The jailer decided to take his own life, but Paul stopped him by shouting that no one had escaped. No one can know what the jailer had heard or known about Paul's message before this event. If he had no previous information, it is a bit peculiar that his first statement to Paul had to do with salvation. There is also an unusual statement that his whole household rejoiced because he had become a believer. The story of the jailer's conversion (and that of his family) was followed by an immediate character transformation in which he began caring for the prisoners by washing their wounds and feeding them.

Acts 16:35-40

Up to this point in the narrative of Acts, nothing had been said about citizenship, but when the magistrates sent an order for Paul and Silas to be released, Paul refused to leave and informed them that they had beaten a Roman citizen, who had also been imprisoned without a trial or a guilty verdict. Some kind of public admission of culpability was necessary, as Paul saw it. This struck fear into the magistrates, for it was illegal to beat a Roman citizen, especially one who had not been condemned. So they came personally and apologized, probably hoping to prevent any further problems. Some have wondered why Paul did not sneak away quietly, but more than personal dignity was at stake. More than likely he knew that there was a need to demonstrate that the little community that he was leaving behind had no stigma on it. After the apology and a request that Paul and Silas leave the city, the mission party went to Lydia's house and stayed long enough to encourage the body of believers. Several times when religious opposition had arisen in the past, the Jews were responsible and had stirred up the native population to exacerbate the problem. This was not the case in Philippi, for the problem was not a religious one. It had been initiated by the native authorities because of economics and revenge. It is also noteworthy that, with this admission by the magistrates, the little community had, in a sense, been declared a *religio licita*, and no further action should be taken against them. Some kind of reason for Paul's refusal to leave secretly had to have been evident to the people of Philippi. He seems to have believed that there was a need to protect those he was leaving behind, and the use of his Roman citizenship served that purpose. The little group in Philippi became a strong force in the Macedonian area, and while they must have suffered further persecution (Phil. 1:29), they came to Paul's aid when he was in Thessalonica by sending a gift. Experiences in a community, whether good or bad, often leave indelible ties, and it is obvious that Paul had a soft spot for this community that must have been reciprocated. Whatever the conflicts, as R.R. Williams has said, "Nothing can stop the gospel. [3].

Acts 17:1-9

The narrative about Philippi was told in the first person (we), but when the party went to Thessalonica, Luke changed to the third person (they). For some reason, he stayed behind. It could have been because Philippi was his hometown. Even without Luke, the same story repeated itself in Thessalonica. Thessalonica was the capital city of Macedonia and was located on the Ignatian Way, about 90 to 100 miles from Philippi. It was a thriving commercial center and enjoyed government by the people, with chosen patriarchs. Paul and Silas went to the synagogue and seemed to have had productive discussions. It has been suggested that Paul changed his method when he entered these Grecian areas. Normally these early meetings could have been described as "teaching," but in this case they were arguing or debating, which would have been what the citizens were accustomed to. But while it may appear to have been a different method, the message was the same.[4] Not only some of the Jews, but many of the devout Greeks, who may have been either God-fearers or proselytes (and, Luke added, "not a few of the leading women"), responded to their preaching. In Thessalonica, the positive response of the Gentiles upset the Jews. With a mob that they created, they developed what appears to have been a riot. That kind of scene had occurred before in some of the Galatian communities.

Acts 17:10-15

This short paragraph shows that there was a vivid interest in Beorea. Luke's designation that the Jews of Beroea were more receptive than those in Thessalonica serves as a transition for Paul's ministry to the great urban centers of Athens and Corinth. The division of the party, sending Paul by ship to Athens and leaving the others behind for a time, may signify more than one normally thinks. The logical reason for leaving Silas and Timothy behind was probably to strengthen the newly formed community while getting Paul, who seems to have been the main object of Jewish opposition, out of the picture. Reasons for sending him away by ship are not stated, but more than likely his life was threatened.

It is always precarious to attempt to "get into the mind" of another person, especially one long deceased. However, if one thinks about it, it is virtually impossible that Paul would not have been concerned. It has already been noted that Tarsus, Paul's hometown, was a stronghold of Stoicism, and since Paul had an inquiring mind, one can hardly see him as uninterested when he was growing up. So as the group of believers put Paul aboard ship, he must have had much time to consider what he was approaching as the ship sailed slowly along the coast. To this author, it seems almost natural, and inevitable, that Paul would have considered the people he was about to engage. For example, the night before I was to have my oral examination for my degree, I was in an intense situation. I had written a thesis entitled, "A Comparative Study of the Concept of Worship in Colossians and Hebrews." I reviewed everything I could, and just before I went to bed, I began to wonder if the professors would ask me to translate a passage from Hebrews. That is not an easy book to translate, so I got up and translated the entire book. It took several hours, but when I had finished I thought I was well-prepared. (It turned out that no one asked me to read a single passage.) The point is that looming confrontations, whether they be friendly or not, present issues for which anyone would want to prepare.

We have no way of knowing how much Greek philosophy Paul had studied, if any. There is definite evidence that he would have at least known he was entering a "lion's den" and must have, at a minimum, considered what his approach would be. (So humor me.) On that slow journey down the coast, did Paul consider the great thought tradition of Athens? If so, he must have known that for more than 600 years, great debates had been waged over some of the issues he would be confronting. The earliest Greek philosophers had been primarily interested in "what the world was made up of." Anyone can examine those debates and find their answers, from Thales (who concluded that everything was made of water) to multiple theories, until finally the conclusion was reached that everything was composed of "atoms," which were invisible and indivisible entities. Since physically severing something was probably the only method of separation, nothing more could be done to analyze matter until new instruments and a new science could be developed. The main thrust then began to deal with metaphysical ideas such as, "What is real?" Perhaps the best example of this came from Plato, who was the famous pupil of Socrates. Two illustrations may help. In a theory which has come to be known as "the Divided Line," Plato postulated that the only reality is the idea. All that we observe is merely a copy (shadow), and behind every entity there is an idea, which is the reality. Such might parallel the idea (dream) in the architect's mind of which the ultimate material building is merely a "shadow copy." This realm of ideas may seem to many to approach what is known as "spirit." What is perhaps Plato's best effort at explaining this metaphysical phenomenon is "The Allegory of the Cave," in which he envisions all humans in a cave, chained so that they cannot turn and can see only the wall in front of them. A fire burns behind them, casting flickering shadows, which are all that they see and know. They never see the real idea, say "horse," but when they see what they call a horse, it is simply a shadow of the real "idea."

Now suppose, by some hook or crook, one prisoner should get free and move out of the cave, beyond the fire and into the sunlight. The experience would be painful, but he would be in the realm of ideas, not shadows. If in some way he made his way back into the cave and tried to explain to the chained characters what he had learned, they would probably consider him a fool. Plato probably believed that only a thinker could ever be able to sense the idea, "good" or "beauty," but what it actually is would be like the shadows — the fire cast on the wall.

After Plato, Aristotle tried to further this metaphysical search by attempting to prove the existence of God. (Not the Hebrew God necessarily, but the supreme being.) Aristotle's clearest argument was that which dealt with "causes" and "effects." Everything has a cause for its being, and behind that cause is another, Much like when one stacks up dominos so that when the first is pushed over the next falls until the end is reached. Finally, one has to jump categories from the last cause to another aspect of cause, such as the wind or a person, as being the push for the beginning of the process of falling. It was Aristotle's logic which would cause one to know that there must, at some point, be a first cause, an "uncaused cause," and that is what we call god. This was the kind of thinking into which Paul was moving and that survived in Athens at least until after the time of Paul.

It would seem from Acts that Luke was not present when Paul was in Athens. This raises the question as to whether the discussion in this chapter of Acts is a reconstruction of the essence of Paul's thought. It is stated in Acts 17:17 that he argued not only in the synagogue, but also in the agora. So there were probably several debates that took place before and/or after the one described in this chapter.

> "Finally, as to Paul's speech, though it can hardly be doubted that in detail it is a free literary creation of the author, the main line taken may well be Paul's own. Its general tone and tenor are exactly what might be expected under the circumstances. There can be no doubt that Paul went to great lengths to find points of contact with his hearers' ways of thinking. . . . Now to the cultured Athenian he strives to demonstrate philosophically that the new revelation of Christian thought is the fulfillment of the religion of reason, common to all mankind."[5]

Since Paul came to Athens by ship, he would have entered through the port of Pireaus. Athens was approximately five miles from the sea, and a long walled corridor had been built connecting it with Pireaus so that the city could not be cut off during a siege. Some of the idols Paul referred to must have been along that route, and the beginning of Paul's address could easily be understood because of so many gods. However, the first efforts he made in Athens were the same as those he had made before, in other synagogues. Yet the discussion also occurred in the agora, where the Athenians were used to hearing debates among the many peripatetics. The two philosophical groups mentioned were the Stoics and the Epicureans. This is not the place to deal with an involved discussion of these two philosophies, but some short explanation must be made so that something of these two teachings, which Paul confronted, may be understood. We must be aware that it is easy to oversimplify the beliefs of these two philosophies, but their ideas contributed to this Athenian debate. It is obvious that the ancient Greek gods were no longer viable for many people.

Zeno of Elia was the founder of the Stoic doctrines. He believed in a god, but it was primarily pantheistic. God is in nature and all things, and humans are emanations from the great spirit. Throughout the history of humanity, nearly everyone has been interested in avoiding as much pain as possible and desirous of sharing pleasure. The strong point of the Stoic thought was its emphasis on virtue as the greatest pleasure. This led to a kind of asceticism and an emphasis on self-control. If virtue is the greatest pleasure, then performance of duty and pursuit of virtue are of most importance. If one steadfastly does what is his duty, then there will be some avoidance of pain, and thus good comes from it. The Stoics emphasized a common brotherhood of humankind, and a sense of determinism. The story is told that a slave of Zeno had stolen something and was about to be punished for that act. The slave said, "But master, according to your teaching I was destined to steal and had no choice in the matter." Zeno is said to have replied, "That is true, but it is also determined that I should punish you."

The Epicureans took a different approach. It is amazing that the reversal of the subject and predicate can produce such different philosophies. Instead of stating that virtue is the greatest pleasure, Epicurius stated that pleasure is the greatest virtue. It is probably correct that Epicurius did not intend for his followers to become hedonists. However, the belief that happiness, or pleasure, is the greatest virtue led to a dearth of prohibitions and regulations and ultimately produced a conclusion that may have been alien to Epicurius' position. There is good evidence that the original intent made a distinction between static and dynamic pleasures. Great pleasure was derived from doing those things that produced long-term pleasure, rather than those indulgencies that produced immediate thrills. Later on in life, those same immediate pleasures could cause damage to one's life and therefore, instead of pleasure, there would be pain. The Epicureans were practical atheists. Even if there were any gods, they were not interested or involved in the affairs of men.

Acts 17:16-34

While there is no archeological evidence of an altar designated "to an unknown god" in this area, such may well have been the case. Other altars have been discovered with dedications to unknown gods, so there is little reason to doubt that

Paul had seen that idea, and the reference to such an inscription became a perfect launching place for his discussion with these philosophers. He could hardly have begun with the simple statement of the *kerygma*, so he started where they were. Since it was common to have debates in the agora, it is not surprising that they would want to hear this new idea Paul was proclaiming. Luke's characterization of the Athenian philosophers, that they were always searching for some new thing, is probably accurate. There is a slightly negative slur in the idea of hearing what this man, who has picked up a bit here and there from other philosophies, would have to say. They did not see him as an original thinker, but as a bit of an eclectic. It was when he mentioned Jesus and the resurrection that they appear to have begun to pay more attention. One would probably miss the point of the introduction of that idea when reading English translations, but it is obvious that they have now discovered what this "seed picker" could say to them. They appear to have thought that he was about to expound on two new deities who were the unknown ones, one the masculine deity and the other his cohort. This is the point at which they seem to have become most interested, when they perceived that he was talking about *Iesous* as the male god and *Anastasis* as the female. The Greek terms would probably have at first simply suggested two new gods. (The term dealing with Jesus is masculine, and the word for resurrection is feminine.) It was not until they understood that by *anastasis* Paul meant life after death that they scoffed at him. Many Greek philosophers did not believe in any personal life after death, but some did support the idea of the immortality of the soul which at the point of physical death was absorbed back into the "all soul." So it seemed ridiculous to them that people could rise from the realm of the dead. Many believe that one of the teachings of the Epicureans was that there could be no life after death.[6] The discussion ended at this point, and even though some of the philosophers wanted to hear more, it seems that there was no further opportunity. In keeping with Paul's sense of mission, it is hard to believe that the entire matter was just dropped, but it did put an end to the discussion in the agora. Luke did not tell us whether more work was done in Athens, but the fact that some were won to the cause would indicate that he continued among those who wanted to hear.

There have been some who believe that Paul's work in Athens was a failure. While his approach was a bit different from any other that we know, there is no reason to think that it was a disaster, for verse 33 states that "some of them joined him and became believers." That group included Dionysius the Areopagite (a member of the ruling council), a woman named Damaris, and others. We have no idea how many followers there may have been. It does not seem quite appropriate to take Paul's statement which he made later, that he had determined to know only Christ and him crucified, as renouncing what he did in Athens. Such an interpretation should also mean that he no longer talked about the resurrection, which is preposterous. The proclamation was not a failure, for some did become believers.

We must remind ourselves that Paul always attempted to begin where his audience was. In this case, he complimented the Athenians on being extremely religious. The translations that call them superstitious do not carry his thought well. The transition from where they were to where Paul wanted to take them was possible because they were constantly searching among their many deities for one who was called the "unknown." Notice how Paul made that step: "For as I went through the city and looked carefully at the objects of your worship, I found among them an altar with the inscription 'To an unknown god.'" (Acts 17:23) This served as a perfect stepping stone, and without insulting them, Paul used it masterfully. He took the opportunity to tell them what they were wishing to know, and he applied his comments to the idea of searching for the one true God. That true God does not need human service in the sense that he lacks anything, and since he was the source of all life, including the human family, Paul was able to link all humanity together. For a Jew to say that kind of thing to Gentiles appears to be a radical approach.

It has been stated that Tarsus, Paul's hometown, was a center of Stoic learning. It is probable that Paul was equipped to discuss the Stoic philosophy, and in Athens he quoted two Stoic poets. The first came from a work of Epimenides, a sixth-century B.C.E. philosopher and poet. (In some information coming from Pausanius, there is reference to a situation where Epimenides, who was a semi-mystical Cretan, during a plague instructed the Athenians to let loose black and white sheep on the Aeropagus, and wherever they stopped to lie down, the Athenians were to offer sacrifices to the god so indicated.) Paul must have known about that long before this debate, for he stated that this unknown, to whom he was pointing them, was "the one in whom we live and have our being." He had their attention, and so he moved to challenge them to repentance and commitment. It was not until he spoke of raising Jesus from the dead that they began to sense that the two things he mentioned, *Iesous* and *anastasis*, were not two new gods, but that he was talking about the outrageous idea that people could rise from the dead.

Acts 18:1-11

Nothing is said about why Paul left Athens and went to Corinth. There does not seem to have been any disturbance as there had been in other places, but for whatever reason he found himself in Corinth, located at the southern end of the isthmus that connects the two portions of Attica. Corinth had been destroyed in 145 B.C.E. but had been rebuilt 100 years later by Julius Caesar. It was a particularly robust economic center, largely because of its location. Sailing around the Hellespont was extremely dangerous from late fall through the winter months, and often maritime traffic almost came to a halt, especially around the southern tip of Achaia. The little isthmus is just about five miles wide, and a causeway had been built from the eastern port of Cenchrea on the Aegean Sea to the western port of Lechaeum. Ships were hauled out of the water, dragged across the causeway, and put back in the water at the Gulf of Lepanto, thus avoiding the Hellespont. (Nero later attempted to build a canal but was unsuccessful. One was not completed until the twentieth century C.E.) That process brought many sailors to the city. The fortress Acrocorinthus towered about 1,400 feet above the city, and on that hill a temple honoring Aphrodite had been constructed. In the temple were about 1,000 prostitutes, and if there ever was any need for encouraging immoral activity, the temple certainly did so. No wonder that a concept synonymous with evil, "to Corinthianize," had developed. Paul must have felt that Corinth provided fertile soil for the gospel, because he stayed for eighteen months with great success. When he arrived he found much in common with a couple who became a great influence in Corinth and later in Ephesus. Nothing is said about whether Aquila and Priscilla were believers when they came to Corinth, but neither is anything said about them being converted and baptized. So most assume that they were already Christians when Paul met them.

Aquila and Priscilla had recently come from Rome because of an edict expelling all Jews from the city. The eviction occurred around 49 C.E., and according to the Roman historian Suetonius, it came about because of a constant uproar over one called "Chrestos," which is most probably a Roman spelling of Christ. This would certainly fit what had happened in other places when Paul had proclaimed Jesus as Messiah. (It is certain that someone had gone to Rome with the message before Paul went to Corinth, even though we have no record of that kind of mission, because there was a Christian community in Rome, and a few years later Paul wrote a letter to them explaining his gospel.) Aquila and Priscilla, who shared a tent-making trade with Paul, became his associates. Priscilla, sometimes called Prisca, appears to have been an especially strong woman, much like Lydia in Philippi, and may have taken the leadership role. As was his custom, on every Sabbath day Paul would enter the synagogue and try to convince both Jews and Greeks.

Soon after, Silas and Timothy joined Paul in Corinth, and he seems to have found new support. Whether some help from Macedonia freed him from daily labor is unknown, but with his new freedom he was able to preach more effectively. Some reaction in the synagogue must have occurred, so he turned to the Gentiles. He first stayed with Titus Justus, whose home was adjacent to the synagogue. The official of the synagogue, Crispus, became a believer, and many Corinthians, presumably Gentiles, responded to the gospel and were baptized. According to his own statements, Paul did not often baptize, but he did baptize Crispus and Gaius and perhaps the household of Stephanus. There is no way of knowing why he did not baptize, but since Silas and Timothy had not yet joined him, he may have found it necessary to perform the rite.

Acts 18:12-17

The coming of Gallio to Corinth is important for the chronology of Paul's life and ministry.[7] Nearly all historians accept that Gallio became proconsul in July 51 C.E., for an inscription in the temple at Delphi states that Gallio became proconsul at the 26th acclamation of the Emperor Claudius. An emperor was understood to rule until his death, but there were many reaffirmations of his office, and the 26th one for Claudius corresponds to C.E. 51 in July. Paul had been in Corinth for some time, so he likely came there in late 50 C.E. That date is accurate within a year, so from it a chronology of Paul's life and activities can be constructed with confidence.

Since Gallio was a new proconsul, the Jews made a disturbance and brought charges against Paul. They apparently hoped for some strong action against him and may have thought that the *religio illicita* issue could be used. But since it became obvious that the charges against Paul had to do with Jewish religious law and not Roman, Gallio rejected the case and indicated that the Jews should take care of it themselves. Gallio was a man of even temperament, and according to his brother, Seneca, he was said to have no vices and especially hated flattery. Seneca also said, "To love him to the utmost was to love him too little," and "No mortal was so sweet to one as he was to all."[8] Of course, the effect was that Paul and Christianity were not denied the right to exist. Some late manuscripts suggest that the Greeks enjoyed seeing Sosthenes, the head of the synagogue, being beaten by the Jews, but that is problematical. The Jews did vent their anger on him and beat him in front of the tribunal, but Gallio disregarded that action, apparently feeling that they were taking care of their own affairs.

It is difficult to be exact about the amount of time Paul spent in Corinth. We know that it was at least eighteen months, and after the events before Gallio we are told that Paul stayed for a "considerable time." With Aquila and Priscilla, he then left Corinth from the seaport of Cenchrea. He later left Aquila and Priscilla, probably in Ephesus, where they must have done a monumental work because when Paul went back to Ephesus, he found a thriving community there.

Two short verses (18:22-23) tell of Paul making a visit to Jerusalem and then going on to Antioch. Those verses were written in the third person, indicating that Luke did not accompany him. Perhaps that accounts for the abbreviated nature of the narrative, since the main purpose was to get on with the issues that the gospel overcame. The time in Jerusalem probably involved the completion of the vow mentioned in verse 18. If it was a Nazarite vow, it would have required the hair to be cut at the beginning of the vow, thirty days before its conclusion, and then to be burned in the temple.[9] In this case Paul's hair would have been offered during the Passover and would confirm his desire to conform to Jewish practices that did not interfere with the gospel of grace, but we have only this short reference and no other information. This may well be another instance where Paul seemed to feel that the new movement was still a part of Judaism, although to him Christianity was the "true Israel." The idea that Paul's presence in Jerusalem would have set off some sort of open hostility, as it did later, is speculation. He was there for only a short time, so it may not have presented any problem. In effect, the return to Antioch would complete the journey he had begun approximately four years before. Luke then stated that after some time Paul returned through Galatia and Phrygia. For the purpose of clarifying these travels and efforts of Paul, the tours have been divided into the first, second, and third missionary journeys, although in all probability Paul did not make that kind of distinction.

[1]R.R.Williams, 122.
[2]Rackham, 282.
[3]Ibid.
[4]Rackham, 295.
[5]G.H.C. Macgregor, *The Interpreter's Bible*, vol. ix (New York-Nashville: Abingdon Press, 1954), 232.
[6]Rackham, 304.
[7]Bruce, 342.
[8]MacGregor, 243.
[9]*The Mishnah*, translated by Herbert Danby (London: Oxford University Press, 1954), 281ff.

Chapter 18

The Ministry in Ephesus

❖

The little interlude in Acts 18 allows time to show how Paul got back to Ephesus and some of what was going on there. He did not slight the churches in Galatia and Phyrgia, but little is said of that ministry. Instead, the narrative returns to Ephesus and introduces a new figure in the story.

Acts 18: 24-19:7

There were groups of early Christians who were not in the mainstream of thought. Already it has been said that there were no written gospels at this time and that the information was passed down through oral tradition. No one can be sure when the "Q" material was compiled or how well-circulated it was, but most scholars place it around 50 C.E., or about the time of Paul's experience. That might mean that the possible lack of accurate information may have led to different understandings. Neither can we tell how many groups there were nor what kinds of materials they circulated. (Keep in mind that we know the eunuch went back to Ethiopia and probably began the Coptic church. Recently, multiple writings which are not canonical have been discovered, and the early community in some places may have used them.) The group that Paul found represents some of the followers of John who had merged some of their teaching with what they knew about Jesus.

The introduction of Apollos into the narrative supports the idea that there was a school of Alexandrian thought that may have been influenced by the kind of thought in Stephen's teaching and in the book of Hebrews. The term "school" does not refer to a formal institution, but a type of thought — just as the thought of John, the apostle, later became dominant around Ephesus. We have no information as to exactly what Priscilla and Aquila found deficient in the teaching of Apollos. Priscilla seems to have taken the lead in this effort. She is mentioned first, which indicates that she was dominant (cf. Romans 16:3, II Timothy 4:19, and Acts 18:2), either because of her rank in society or because of her abilities.[1] It should also be evident that at this time there was no discrimination regarding females taking the lead. Even though Apollos was a highly educated man, he was willing to take instruction from Priscilla and Aquila, indicating a certain humility and a lack of dogmatism on his part. After this instruction, Apollos went to Corinth, where he became an important teacher. He appears to have not only been brilliant, but eager and able to persuade others of his view of Messiah-ship. The twelve disciples whom Paul found, who knew only the baptism of John, once again suggests how diverse some of the groups of believers were. They do not appear to have perpetuated a "John the Baptist" sect, for they were followers of Jesus. Paul's question relative to their reception of the Spirit and the answer that they gave shows that they did not even know that the promised Paraclete had come in the lives of the believers. Again, those promises which were made most evident in the fourth gospel may not as yet have been circulated. It also implies that their information had not come through the same line of thought as that in Acts. At any rate, since the baptism of John was a preparatory one and was done in reference to (*eis*) the forgiveness of sins, they were baptized with Christian baptism and received the presence of the Holy Spirit. (The preposition *eis* seems to have always meant "with particular reference to" something. It may be unfortunate theologically that it was translated "for" in early English translations. Bruce indicated that this is the only case we have of "re-baptism," but this baptism was with a completely different meaning and was not actually re-baptism.[2] Paul explained that Christian baptism has a unique meaning because it refers first to the death and resurrection of Jesus, and then it is said to portray the death of the believer to sin/self and the resurrection to or beginning of a new kind of life. There is no distinct order in Acts for the reception of the Spirit, for in the case of Cornelius it came before baptism, showing the approval of Gentile entrance into the church.

As was his custom, Paul began his work in Ephesus by going to the synagogue. Whether others had gone before him is unknown, but to our knowledge, most of them were Gentiles, so Paul's efforts may have been the first to the Jews. He seems to have had more success than he had experienced in other cities, for he was able to make his argument concerning the kingdom of God for some time. We have no record concerning how long he taught about the kingdom in the synagogue in Ephesus, but something in his message led to a rupture. One can only surmise that some Jews reacted negatively to his emphasis on the inclusive nature of the kingdom. When their resistance became stronger, they began to malign the Way. Paul and the Jews who had become believers left the synagogue, and for the next two years he taught in the lecture hall of Tyrannus. (There does not seem to have been any major issue among the Jews until Paul came on the scene.) Some ancient authorities add that he lectured from eleven o'clock in the morning until four in the afternoon. If that is correct, he probably labored at the tent-making tasks during the early morning hours while Tyrannus used the hall before eleven. Usually, labor was suspended during the time Paul is said to have taught, and it probably was a time of leisure, when the people would have been available.[3] The note that both Jews and Greeks heard the message would indicate a thriving success.

Acts 19:8-20

The ancient world was filled with magic spells and incantations, and most people seemed to have believed that the invisible world was characterized by evil. This was true in the Jewish world, and it certainly affected the Gentile world in which Paul found himself. Paul attributed all of the good things that happened in Ephesus to God, for he saw God working to bring about positive results in the lives of those who were sick, both physically and spiritually. Even in the modern world, we still have not been able to determine how much impact a positive faith has on physical well-being. We do know that a calm, confident, serene spirit can help to overcome stress and thus help with ulcers, heart issues and mental despair. Earlier in Acts, we have seen times when people longed for Peter's shadow to fall on them, and in the passage before us Luke told of those who took handkerchiefs, towels, or aprons that Paul had touched and used them to help heal the sick.

Whether that was what moderns would call psychological is really unimportant, especially since the mind-body relationship is still with us. That there were professional exorcists is beyond doubt, and if they could find a source to enhance their power of exorcism, which many respected, it would certainly solidify their position. Therefore, because of the transforming effect that Jesus had on the lives of so many, the seven sons of Sceva decided to cash in on that power. But the man they meant to cure turned on them with fury; the "evil spirit" using the voice and body of the man overpowered them, and they fled in fear. This caused many who had committed themselves to the gospel that Paul was preaching, but who maintained some interest in the accepted magic, to abandon magic and destroy their magic aids. The value of the material destroyed is hard to ascertain. Luke does not say what the coins were, but probably the value of a silver coin would have been about one day's wage. Inflation and depression cycles change the value of any currency, but perhaps the best estimate would be, assuming about 300 working days in a year, that 50,000 coins would represent about 160 to 170 years annual wages.

The time spent in Ephesus must have been around 53-56 C.E., during which Paul may have written a number of letters. It is not possible or necessary to examine all of them, but all of the Corinthian Correspondence must belong to this period, and problems plaguing the Corinthian community disturbed Paul to no end. Since we are looking at the major issues that threatened the gospel, we now turn to that material, primarily in what we call I Corinthians and a few portions of II Corinthians.

[1] Bruce, 342-354.
[2] Ibid.
[3] Stagg, 200.

Chapter 19

The Nature of the Corinthian Correspondence

Although the entire Corinthian Correspondence has long been looked at as inspired scripture (and with good cause), at the outset they were simple letters. In some cases, they were personal communications; in others, they were addressed to the specific problems of a person, group, or church. Paul probably never thought that they would become scripture for the future church, but often the purposes and works of God are mysterious, unexpected, and unforeseen to the human intellect. However, the nature of this set of materials needs to be seen in the light of the problems which are described and seen as a threat to the Corinthian church. In everything that we call scripture, there seems to be first an immediate application, then some principle that comes from it and that is valid for all times. Perhaps the formal term "epistles" has often prevented the intensely personal atmosphere of these letters from being seen.

The city of Corinth was a tremendously important economic center. Its location at the southern end of the isthmus connecting the two sections of Achaia made it inevitable that the bulk of the north-south trade would pass through the city. (Some of this has already been discussed, but it is so important that it needs to be re-examined.) The isthmus was about five miles across, and it separated the sea on the eastern port of Cenchrea from the gulf of Corinth on the west. That gulf joined what is now known as the Gulf of Patrai, which emptied into the Ionian Sea. Its importance was intensified because of the dangers related to shipping around the Cape of Malea, a treacherous body of water. Two methods were devised to avoid the roughly 200 miles around the cape, especially in the winter. The first dealt with the capacity of Corinth to unload ships and transport their cargo overland to the other side of the isthmus. Obviously, this was a time-consuming and laborious task, but it made the bustling city even more active, with sailors on shore leave while those operations were taking place. The second method involved the causeway, which was built so that ships could be drawn out of the water, moved overland (pulled by animals), and put back in the water on the other side.

In either case, many of those things contributed to the atmosphere of the city, and when the Temple to Aphrodite is added to the mix, corruption was almost inevitable. There were both male and female prostitutes attendant to the temple, and by the very nature of prostitution the "trade" was pursued after hours. The population in general had accepted the situation and the apparent approval of the dominant religion's immorality. When Paul came to Corinth around 50/51 C.E., he spent more than a year and a half there. That portion of Paul's work has already been discussed, but the church in Corinth was extremely young and had multiple problems which had to be dealt with. So when Paul came back, probably to Ephesus, he received some information that demanded a response. It is probable that while he was in Ephesus, he wrote to address those issues.

What we currently call I Corinthians was not the first of the letters, which means that the Corinthian Correspondence, as we have it, is not in its proper order. This may be the result of the difficulty of preserving documents written on fragile papyrus, or, since these documents were not considered "holy," there may have been no effort to keep them in their chronological order. It has long been recognized that I Corinthians 5:9 contains a reference to a previous letter. So from Paul's own statement, what we know as I Corinthians was not the first communication. The general consensus is that tucked away in II Corinthians is a passage that interrupts the flow of that letter and is perhaps at least a portion of the first (lost) letter. If one reads II Corinthians without what is here called an insert, the flow of ideas is not interrupted:

> II Corinthians 6:11: "We have spoken frankly to you, Corinthians, our heart is open to you. There is no restriction in our affections, but only in yours. In turn, I speak to you as children, open wide your hearts also. (omission of the insert) 7:2: Make room in your hearts for us; we have wronged no one, we have taken advantage of no one. I do not say this to condemn you, for I said before that you are in our hearts, to die together and to live together."

Corinthians "A"

When that passage is read (especially read aloud), the flow is so smooth without the insert that its absence is not noticeable. The conclusion reached here, which agrees with most scholarship, is that a portion of the first letter was attached at this point because of broken papyrus sheets or perhaps for some other reason. There is no manuscript evidence to support the theory, but (in all probability) it was done before any of our extant manuscripts were written. That would identify the insert as at least a portion of the first letter which referred to in I Corinthians 5:9. For our purposes, the insert will be called Corinthians "A."

Corinthians "B"

This will be used to designate what we know as I Corinthians. It was written in answer to certain information Paul had received from several sources: Chloe's people, whomever they may have been; Fortunatus, Stephanus and Achaius; and from questions in a letter that the church sent asking for Paul's advice. Since we do not have the letter, we must try to reconstruct that side of the conversation. The response to Paul's letter was not good. Things actually got worse, and it is probable that Paul made a personal visit, because a third visit was proposed in II Corinthians 13:1-2.

Corinthians "C"

After his visit, Paul must have written what is called the severe letter, which is now II Corinthians 10-13. That portion of the correspondence indicates that the conflicts were still unsolved, and that Paul seems to have felt that the letter was too harsh and regretted sending it. (II Corinthians 7:8) Who has not posted a letter in the midst of a misunderstanding and then had second thoughts? As the material stands in the presently accepted order, it seems to be a reversal of the situation in II Corinthians 1-9, where all of the issues are solved. But in the present order they reappear in II Corinthians 10-13. Therefore, the most logical conclusion is that II Corinthians 10-13 is the severe letter, which would have been written before the first nine chapters of what is currently called II Corinthians. Paul was so anxious about the situation that he set out to meet Titus (who was the bearer of the letters). When they met, the news was good. The Corinthians had accepted Paul's solution. The problems were solved.

Corinthians "D"

This piece of the correspondence represents our II Corinthians 1-9 without the insert (6:14-7:1). At this point everything seems to be settled.

Chapter 20

Some of the Problems at Corinth

Since the major issues that confronted the Corinthian church are addressed in the letter we call I Corinthians, they will be dealt with in detail, with the remainder of the correspondence to be touched on incidentally. It was almost inevitable that when the gospel message hit the Gentile world, there would be issues (mountains to move) between the Gentiles and the Jews. The demands of the gospel also confronted a different culture and way of life. To transform them could hardly have happened without conflicts, both inwardly with each person and socially. The letter begins with an address to people who are called "saints," which is not a designation of some "super" Christian as it is in modern thought. In the New Testament, every committed Christian is uniquely set apart and, therefore, a saint. They are recognized for their spiritual endowment and for the awareness of their spiritual gifts. They are also commended for their patient waiting for the "Day of the Lord Jesus Christ" and encouraged to understand that God is faithful, however long the intervening time may be. Lurking in the background of the New Testament writings is the expectation of a quick return of Christ.

I Corinthians 1:1-9

The first issue to be dealt with had to do with divisions that had sprung up in the church. The discussion starts in I Corinthians 1:10 and goes through much of Chapter 4. Obviously, that sort of division is not consistent with the fellowship of believers and the concept of the church as "The Body of Christ." The idea of no dissension does not mean that there can be no difference of opinion, but rather that the fellowship of the body demands unity of purpose. Cliques, such as the ones described in this section, develop out of dogmatism.

Some of the Problems at Corinth

I Corinthians 1:10-4:40

We are not provided information about Chloe's people, but apparently they were the source of the information about people being divided into cliques and following different teachers. (The letter giving the information may have pointed out who they were, or the group may have been small enough that everyone knew who they were, especially Paul.) Such followings should not be a surprise to modern readers, for the temptation to follow charismatic leaders is evident, not only among denominations but also in regard to media preachers. The issue will be ongoing unless egos are sublimated and people begin to understand that all servants of Christ are merely tools used in Christ's service. At least three groups, maybe four, are identified, and Paul defines them as being followers of three teachers. Since Paul was the one who first brought the gospel message to Corinth and appears to have been the founder of the church, there would have been those whose lives had been changed because of his ministry, and they would be forever grateful. That is normal and can never be ignored. The second teacher they exalted was Apollos. When he first appeared in Ephesus, he was described as a brilliant person and a gifted orator. Some would have been swayed by his rhetoric, especially if his ability surpassed that of Paul. The third one mentioned is Peter. We know that he was a stalwart leader of the early church, and there is reason to believe that he had either visited the Corinthian church or that they knew of his reputation. None of this suggests that any of these men were responsible for the divisions, but that the people had allowed themselves to focus on the servants rather than the master.

Paul also said that there were some who said, "I belong to Christ." It is possible that this group took a superior attitude; by claiming that they belonged to Christ, they implied that others did not. The primary issue is that following Christ is not following any man. There had been no baptism in the names of Paul, Apollos, or Peter, and thus any party loyalty such as that suggested here is a contradiction to the faith. Paul seems to have been determined to show them that while eloquence is good, or while the position of a primary apostle is honorable, they must not create divisiveness over these men. Every servant should always wish to do his or her best, but the temptation to self-importance must be rigorously resisted, for the loyalty belongs to Christ and not to any servant.

Party spirit is also inconsistent with the nature of the true gospel. The wisdom of the gospel is not that of the world. In fact, the crucifixion death of Jesus at first appeared to be foolishness, for who could ever believe that a condemned criminal, as the world would see it, could ever produce anything in terms of spirituality? But wisdom had failed to know God, probably because God is beyond the scope of logic, and while philosophers and teachers can state their understanding of God, no one has ever been able to prove or disprove his existence or understand the spiritual realm. While all attempts to understand God are of value, he is beyond human ability to understand. The Jewish people looked for signs, and while there have been many things that can be seen in that light, still any of them can be dismissed as coincidence. As it is seen in this work, there is nothing in Paul's thinking that is against intellect "per se." But still, as the writer of Hebrews says, "without faith (commitment) it is impossible to please God."

The Corinthian church appears to have included many who were from various levels of understanding and education. Perhaps some, but not many, belonged to the "wise" category and some belonged to the aristocracy, but none of that ultimately mattered to Paul, who did not believe that any human position was grounds for boasting. The only attitude that is proper in the Christian framework is gratitude. Once again, let it be understood that Paul's reference to his work in Athens (I Corinthians 2:1-2) did not in any way renounce the value of that experience. The position in this work is that some of the most renowned scholars, to whom the greatest respect is owed, have missed the point of the value of his Athenian ministry. The Athenian discourse had begun where the people were and had led them to the *kerygma*.[1] Just as there should be no arrogance because of one's ability, there should also be no premium on ignorance. Jesus had indicated to his disciples, in regard to their coming conflicts, that they should depend on God to give them a defense.

This is sometimes used to suggest that study and preparation are not needed. Such a suggestion is a misapplication of what Jesus said because it does not take into consideration the specific time, issues, and purpose of that discourse. Paul's statement here seems to renounce any arrogance that supplants the central story. His fear was that he himself would be seen in his own power rather than in his real concern that he was weak without the power of God's spirit. It had nothing to do with feeling that the Athenian message was a mistake. For Paul, any wisdom that ignores faith and reliance on God is like the wisdom of the world. The passage that states, "What no eye has seen nor ear heard, nor human heart conceived, what God has prepared for those that love Him, these things God has revealed through His Spirit," may refer to the things of the ultimately real world — that is, of the heavenly, spiritual realm as contrasted with the things of the visible, material world. Natural wisdom, regardless of how valuable it may be, cannot compare with the wisdom given by the Holy Spirit.

Just as party spirit is inconsistent with the fellowship of believers (the Body of Christ) and with the nature of the gospel itself, it is also inconsistent with the proper conception of Christian workers and their work. At least for Paul, there was a responsibility to take the spiritually immature and lead them beyond self-centered, human attitudes. (Augustine once said, "Without *agapé* even the Greek virtues become splendid vices.") So the spirit of those taking the party–spirit line was an egocentric, self-contained and self-directed attitude that was and is inconsistent with the nature of the gospel. For a Christian worker (Paul, Apollos, or any other) the concern should never be "what I have done." Remember: Paul planted, Apollos watered, but God brought in the crop.

The apostle attempted to show the Corinthians that laying the wrong kind of foundation (which should never be on any human but on Christ), or building with the wrong kind of materials, would fall sort in the ultimate test. He introduced the noble idea of each Christian being the temple of the Holy Spirit and that any work done is simply done as stewards.

In the latter part of this section, he attempted to show that everything belongs to Christ and that nothing belongs to the servants except the privilege of service. Everything Paul said about himself, Apollos, or anyone else had been for the benefit of the Corinthians. It had not been meant as a criticism in regard to those servants. This answer to the issue of divisiveness ends with a bit of sarcasm. Some of the Corinthians seem to have gained wealth and become haughty. On the other hand, the apostles appear to stand in need and in weakness, and are expendable. He contrasted the apostles with the Corinthians as weak versus strong, or fools versus the wise, and suggested that the apostles were almost refuse in this world. Then, he admonished them to follow his example, and suggested that when he did come there would be a reckoning. The atmosphere of a future visit would be determined by their response.

[1]William Barclay, *The Letters to the Corinthians*, rev. ed. (Philadelphia: Westminster Press, 1975), 23, 24.

Chapter 21

Matters Necessitating Discipline

I Corinthians 5:1-13

The first of these issues, whether the information was sent to Paul in the letter or came from some other source, had to do with sexual immorality. Considering the cultural and social atmosphere of Corinth, this kind of issue would certainly arise. It is difficult to be certain about the offense from the information we have, but it would appear that the problem was an illicit relationship of a man living with his stepmother, and the church does not appear to have been concerned about it. That kind of response, or lack of one, suggests tacit approval of the situation.

> "Shocked as he was at the sin, Paul was even more shocked at the attitude of the Corinthian church toward the sinner. They had complacently accepted the situation and had done nothing about it when they should have been grief stricken. The term that Paul uses for the grief they should have shown is the word that was used for mourning for the dead *penthrin*. An easy going attitude toward sin is always dangerous."[1]

Remember the Jerusalem letter (Acts 15), in which one of the things the Gentiles were warned about was fornication? The correction Paul suggested here dealt only with the man, which causes one to suspect that the woman was not a Christian. Such things may not have been uncommon in this city, and the infant church may have been in a quandary as to how to proceed. To allow such conduct to go unchallenged would weaken the moral stance of the community; therefore, action was imperative. It must be remembered that in Jesus' discussion on discipline in Matthew 18:15-17, the primary focus was on the recovery of the offending member. That discussion dealt with one member of the community offending (sinning against) another member and not this kind of immoral behavior. Still, in this kind of extreme situation, the effort should always be to help the individual become aware of the unacceptable actions, and if he/she persists in that action, he/she will, in a sense, actually remove himself/herself from the body.

Paul had previously written about problems with sexually immoral persons (I Corinthians 5:9). The issue had not been with all sins, but specifically with the attitude toward the sexual problems with which the church had been linked. Paul appears to have believed that close association with those outside the church whose lives were characterized by the evils he mentioned would endanger the entire community. It was not possible for them to judge or advise about the actions of those who were not a part of the church, but they should not offer tacit approval of such behavior and thus become a part of it. It is extremely difficult to know how to deal with such problems in the modern age, especially in terms of pronouncing judgment on others, but the principle is still applicable: Be careful that a little yeast does not affect the whole. Whatever this "handing the man over to Satan" may have meant, it certainly emphasizes the idea that the church must be diligent about the lives of its people and its reputation.

I Corinthians 6:1-8

The second problem in this series had to do with lawsuits before heathen courts. The situation is somewhat different in the modern world, where a distinction between pagan courts and those in our society must be made. As is true with most scripture, we must extract a principle from this discussion, taking into consideration that modern courts are often run by judges who are not pagan and that the system itself is based on moral law. Lawyers and other court officials are often Christians, but that was not the case in ancient Greece. Even so, Paul's advice is applicable. There should be few cases where one Christian takes another to court, for when that happens the entire movement comes under scrutiny and the Christian influence may be harmed. But such action in Corinth would recognize a power higher than the morality of the Christian gospel and therefore should be avoided whenever possible. Once, when this author was minister in a small community, two Christian men whose farms adjoined had a serious disagreement. One of them had built a small dam on his property, and during an unusual storm the creek backed up and destroyed a portion of the other man's cotton crop. The argument between the two escalated until finally a suit was filed. Though the men were not members of the same church, they were viewed as Christian brothers, and therefore the entire community, as well as the fellowship of the two men, was damaged. Which is more important, to gain "justice" at the expense of the Body of Christ or to suffer some loss, if that suffering would help promote forgiving in a Christian atmosphere?

Even though the thrust of Paul's gospel was that salvation came by faith and not through works, he strongly believed that those who were consistently characterized as "wrongdoers" were not people who had experienced that grace (I Corinthians 6:9-11). His primary concern was that in these cases the Christian community was acting no differently than the pagan one. The principle in this instance seems to be that when the Christian community allows itself to be judged by pagan courts, it admits to and recognizes a higher authority. Therefore, in the church, one should submit to the spirit of love rather than the spirit of rights. For Paul, any case brought into a heathen court indicates a failure in the brotherhood and probably indicates a failure involving influence. He gave no advice in this passage about conflicts with those outside the community; in those cases, one must examine himself/herself and the motives involved in terms of Christ-like character. Neither does this apply to the processes of dealing with insurance companies and other modern issues that may require litigation.

I Corinthians 6:9-20

One of the problems that sometimes accompanies the gospel of salvation by faith is the danger of abuse by suggesting that behavior does not matter. As long as one followed the legalistic concept of justification by following the legal precepts, there was always the possibility and threat that if one disobeyed the commandments, certain punishment was to follow. When that restraint is taken away with apparently nothing to replace it, the danger is that the libertarian thought that one can do with impunity anything he/she chooses will take over. Christianity has found it necessary to battle this twisted thinking, and it of necessity involves the concept of the Lordship of Christ as the motivating factor to be Christ-like in action. When that gospel was placed in Greece (especially in Corinth, where lax behavior was a norm) along with the idea that humankind was trapped in a material body, which is distinct from its soul (the body was seen as evil "per se"), it is easy to see that for many, two options were available: one could either follow a rigid asceticism and deny the body, or argue that the body really made no difference and one could allow the bodily appetites to run unchecked. In the face of those options, Paul argued for a new kind of ethic. It may be correct that "all things are lawful," but all things are not helpful. The apostle attempted to show that he was not willing to be dominated by any of his bodily appetites. He had often dealt with the concept that one is "in Christ," and therefore his entire being is united to the Lord. To give control of the body to one's desires, or to unite with a prostitute, is to violate that oneness with the Lord. Apparently, such dominant thoughts vied for the control of the Corinthian congregation and threatened to destroy the unique challenge of being committed to Christ as Lord. It is a rather unusual idea that fornication is a sin against one's own body and that other sins are outside the body. One could argue that there are other issues that are against one's body, such as drunkenness or drug addiction, but the primary mountain that the Corinthians faced was that of sexual perversion. Therefore, the entire argument hinges on the fact that "you have been bought with a price; therefore, glorify God in your body."

The focus of the argument is sexual (6:12-20), but the implications reach farther. Paul has just finished naming the numerous characterizations of "outsiders," and they have not been limited to sex. Christians have been liberated and therefore must have a new concept of responsibility. If one is united to Christ, he/she is one with him and with fellow members of the body in any action. Any of those actions would affect the body, whether the action is good one or is contrary to Christ's teaching or spirit, such as any anti-*agapé* spirit or action that would violate the body. The body is the temple of the Lord. The principle is, "you are not your own."

[1]William Barclay, *The Letters to the Corinthians* (Philadelphia: Westminster Press, 1976), 44.

Chapter 22

Specific Questions from Corinth

❖

Beginning in Chapter 7 of I Corinthians and reaching to the end of the letter, except for the final division, Paul offered advice concerning the questions the Corinthian church had asked. Since this work is concerned with the many questions and mountains that the gospel had to overcome, this letter is vital. Even though these are local questions, they probably harassed the entire Christian community. Although we often think that the Corinthian community presented an intensity of evil, there is good reason to believe that many of these issues were common in the Gentile world, so much of Paul's advice would be applicable in all communities. But since these particular issues were brought to the front by the Corinthian church, no adamant claim can be made that these same issues prevailed in Ephesus, Philippi, or any of the other churches in Asia, Greece, or even in Italy. However, the principles imbedded in the answers would have been valuable for all of the churches and even the modern world.

I Corinthians 7:1-9

The first question must have dealt with many issues related to marriage. Nearly all of the answers must be seen in the light of the dominant thought in first- century expectations — that is, that the end of the age was eminent. One can hardly study the New Testament seriously without sensing that issue, for wherever the gospel was preached, the quick return of the Lord was expected. Therefore, some of the answers would apply in Corinth in a way that they might not in the modern church. In that light, Paul answers certain questions about the marital state in Chapter 7, but he begins by suggesting that it would be better if all sexual experiences could be avoided. But even as he believed that the end was near, he also was highly practical, and because of the strong biological sexual urges, he knew that, in most cases, marriage was much better than remaining single.

This is not a strange idea for those who are ascetically inclined; it has happened in many religious communities. But his advice regarding celibacy should never be taken to imply that the celibate state is in any way more holy than the married state. For most people, celibacy is unnatural, but for some, it may have an attraction. At one point, Jesus had indicated that there were some who were eunuchs from birth, but he also knew that some had undergone castration and chosen to be eunuchs. In the discussion of the story of the Ethiopian eunuch, it was stated that the Jewish religious system looked rather askance at any sexual mutilation, except circumcision, and also it is evident that marriage was expected. But any attempt to argue that the non-married state is superior is not in keeping with Paul's thought. He even stated that there should be abstinence between husband and wife for specific times and purposes, which was his own conclusion and not "of command." He did appear to hint that whatever his condition was, he could wish that all might share it. Since Paul had most likely been a member of the Sanhedrin, we can only guess what his marital condition had been and was. Being a Sanhedrin member required that one should be married and have at least one child. Yet during the time of his ministry as we know it, Paul had no family responsibilities, which would have been a good thing for a missionary who was constantly on the move. There is a principle of marriage relative to these answers. While the "two become one," they are still individuals involved in commitment, and each should be aware that their bodies are not just their own. The responsibility is to be aware of the needs of the other. It would be hard to believe that a trained rabbi would understand that God's creation, with its strong reproductive desires, could be in any sense evil. However, with the end expected in some immediate sense, the advice may be tempered by that concept.

Paul also indicated that the unmarried and widows would be better off if they remained single. Again, this idea probably reflects the expectation of the immediate return of the Lord., but even under those circumstances Paul did not speak against marriage. It is true that marriage responsibilities can carry burdens, such as those that plagued William Carey when his wife refused to understand his challenge to go to India and did not go with him. But it is also true that a good wife or husband can offer support and encouragement to the partner and make him/her much stronger. Whatever one may think regarding the inspiration of the scripture, in these passages Paul is only offering his opinions.

I Corinthians 7:10-24

Paul's teaching for those who are unmarried is consistent with the teaching of Jesus that marriage is sacred and should be held in highest regard. However, the issue of divorce has been a difficult one, and the church has not been able to develop a consistent position on it. Most would admit that marriage takes diligent work and that the union should be a lifetime commitment. But there are issues, such as abuse, that were not recognized in the first century, and some of them may offer just cause for divorce. A professional counselor was once discussing with this author a case in which both were involved. The counselor said, "You are trying to save a marriage, but I am trying to save a person." He was right, and his comment was an eye-opener. It is easy to see that if, in Corinth, one partner became a Christian and the other did not (which must have been almost inevitable), it might create a situation in which, if the unbeliever chose to separate, there was no longer a binding responsibility on the believer. That is a reason beyond the exception given by Jesus, but it makes sense, and was the position Paul took. However, it was Paul's hope that the believing spouse could influence the other by remaining faithful, and that remaining in the relationship could dignify the lives of the children. (It would be a complete contradiction to Paul's understanding of the gospel to suggest that he taught that one person's faith could save another.) But failing all efforts to preserve the union, Paul stated that the believer was no longer bound. (There is an apocryphal tale already referred to in this work, *The Acts of Paul and Thecla*, which indicates that Paul was in trouble in Asia because some thought he was trying to prevent or destroy marriages. Even though that work has little validity, if any, it does show the possibility that there were those who felt that Paul was an enemy of marriage, and it might be easy for some to draw that conclusion.) In these pieces of advice, Paul took the position that everyone should be content with his/her situation. This did not mean that if a slave was offered the possibility of manumission, he should not take advantage of it, but Paul did not see Christianity as a radical revolution, socio-political or otherwise. Paul dealt with this issue in a little letter to Philemon, whose runaway slave had become a Christian. Paul took the position that he was returning the slave but that now Philemon must treat him as a brother, which would be impossible to do and still keep him in the "slave" category. What Paul's advice did was to "cut off" the legs on which slavery stood so that it would ultimately collapse. Again, that position relative to revolution may reflect the belief in the early return of Jesus, but it says nothing about liberation theology, including the position of women or other social movements based on Christian principles.

I Corinthians 7:25-40

A more pressing issue was: What should be done in the case of unmarried people? Paul plainly stated that because of the "impending crisis" they should remain as they were. But once again, there was no hint that there was anything wrong in marrying, and for the sake of preserving the race and even the church, it is good that few paid attention to what Paul said. As Paul saw it, the primary issue facing believers was an effort to help people avoid distress. His belief that an unmarried man was free from cares about his family and that an unmarried woman could devote herself more freely to the Lord was not written as a regulation, but as something he personally believed. It is difficult to decide who the "virgins" in this passage were. Were they already engaged to be married, or were they daughters who should not be given in marriage? (Giving in marriage reflects the ancient idea that all members of the family are the property of the father.) Some have interpreted this passage as one that concerned the father of the virgin. The latter part of the chapter seems to deal with the couple rather than their parents. The translation used as the basis for this work (the NRSV) treats this issue as being a decision for the couple and has no reference to the parents. Paul's reference to widows, and we would also consider widowers, indicates that they would be free to marry, but considering the condition of the first-century world as Paul saw it, they should not marry unbelievers. For Paul, marriage was not a sinful or lesser state, even though his opinion was that a single life was better. This was his opinion, and he believed it was in harmony with the Spirit.

Chapter 23

Idolatry and Related Problems

I Corinthians 8:1-13

In discussing this advice to the Corinthians, one must keep in mind the terrific struggle that produced James' conclusion about restrictions that should be sent to the Gentile churches (Acts 15). The argument really began over what constituted salvation and, except for some side remarks and the fact that the issue was hardly mentioned, it became obvious that the apostolic understanding was that Gentiles did not have to become Jewish proselytes to be Christian. However, the numerous problems discussed in the document related to the issue of how Jewish Christians could have fellowship with Gentile Christians, and one of them dealt with meeting the issue of idolatry head-on. Beginning with Moses, there was a warning about making any images of God or gods. Those earliest positions did not deal with monotheism, but rather seemed to take the henotheistic position that there may be many gods, but there is only one for us. That warning was often disregarded by the people, and there is evidence that they fell into idolatry on numerous occasions. Idolatry became a major issue with the eighth-century monotheistic prophets, and the prevailing thought was that idolatry had been the major contributing factor in the disastrous exile. It was thus strongly forbidden. So it should be expected that when the Jewish segment of Christianity saw any association with people who worshipped idols, they saw a "red flag." As a result, the letter in Acts 15 admonished Gentile Christians not to share in idolatry in any way, especially in eating meat that had been sacrificed to an idol. The assumption was that such meats were contaminated, and anyone who ate them was sharing in idolatry. That letter was sent in 49 C.E. and may have been primarily addressed to the Galatian churches. How far-reaching it was is unknown, but it is never alluded to in this information to the Corinthians.

The principle with which Paul began this argument is that everyone possesses some knowledge, but reliance on knowledge alone creates egotism. Therefore, for the Christian, the most important underlying factor for behavior is *agapé*. This will also play a large part in his discussion later about confusion and chaos in public worship. Actually, he insists that idols have a pseudo-existence. For believers, there can be only one pivotal value, only one God, and therefore all idol worship is false and imaginary. Yet pseudo-existence or not, idols do have a reality of influence, and not every person understands the issue of "pseudo." Paul knew that in the Christian community there were some who still had qualms about eating meats offered to idols. The major emphasis in this passage brings into focus the meaning and significance of sin. If one is actually committed to Christ as *Lord*, but deep down in his/her conscience there is a belief that eating these meats is contrary to Jesus' will, then to eat them is sin, whether doing so is actually wrong or not. That would apply to anything. To take a ludicrous example, if one believes that chewing gum or drinking coffee is a sin (to take what most would see as an amoral issue, at least until someone spits out a wad of chewed gum and it gets on the bottoms of my shoe), then chewing gum is sin. *It is not the thing itself, but the violation of one's conscience about the sovereignty of Christ over his/her life.* Once, during the civil rights struggle, this author was ministering in a rural church in an area where racial feeling was strong. One day, in a discussion, one of the church leaders avowed, "I don't care if Jesus himself tells me to let 'niggers' [his term, not mine] into this church, I am not going to do it." I shuddered from head to toe. I certainly did not agree with his position, but if he had simply said that he did not think that it was right for the races to worship together, I would have understood and respected that. I have no way of knowing whether he realized the scope of his statement, but when he said that he would deliberately violate the will of Christ, he *indicated a disregard for the Lordship of Christ, and that was wrong.*

For Paul, it would appear that eating or not eating meats sacrificed to idols was meaningless, but the over-riding issue was the conscience involved. Take a hypothetical example. Suppose that a first-century Christian family decides to host a dinner for fifty fellow church persons. The issue becomes an economic one. Everyone knows that steak is costly, say $4 a pound, but bologna is cheap at 50 cents a pound. The dinner will be costly if we serve steak, but who wants to be served baloney? Then someone makes a remarkable discovery; Ari's meat market is selling steak for $2 a pound. The only hitch is that Ari has a brother who is a priest in the temple of Aphrodite, and he gets the leftover meat and sells it at a greatly reduced price in Ari's store. Who cares? So the family decides to get their meat through Ari and save a bundle. When the meal is held, everyone is enjoying it tremendously and the fellowship is great. Then someone says, "This is the best meat I have ever eaten. Where did you get it?" Mr. Stephanopolis is in the process of swallowing another delicious bite when he hears the answer: "It came from Ari's." Now everyone knows where Ari gets his meat, and Mr. Stephanopolis has a strong conscience about eating meat that has been sacrificed to an idol. He can't spit it out — it has gone too far. So this good Christian family, which intended this meal to be a great fellowship experience, has just caused Mr. Stephanopolis to violate his conscience, and in doing so they have destroyed a part of the fellowship. (Of course, the nut who asked where it came from should not have asked such a question.) Which should be more important, the respect for another's conscience, economics, or personal liberty?

To be sure, Paul's description of those who can't eat such meat as "weak" implies strongly that he sees their position as not correct, but still their consciences should be honored. So he concludes with a principle that suggests that honoring consciences and the fellowship was much more important than one's own liberty. That immediately creates a correct answer, but it also poses another question: How far will I allow the weakness of another to control my behavior? The question will require a case by case answer by each individual. For instance, in the search for truth, some who may go farther than others. In fact, there are those who believe that the intellectual study of religion is evil and should be avoided at all costs. Should the possibility even be considered that the search should be stopped? Every action, even drinking coffee, may have those who believe it is evil, so each individual will have to protect his/her awareness of the other's conscience.

Paul's conclusion in I Corinthians 8:13 still stands as the best answer to these dilemmas. "If eating meat is the cause for others falling, I will not eat meat so that I may not cause one of them to fall." Two major problems thus accompany the Christian on his/her journey: a) Every act or attitude that I am involved in has in it a responsibility regarding influence. b) Although I may be liberated from some taboos, I must always consider my brother's conscience. In effect, Paul has implied that the letter from the Jerusalem conference was not binding on him, but at the same time he spent chapters 9 and 10 using illustrations and rabbinic arguments to show that he strenuously attempted to avoid the use of personal liberty which might violate another believer's freedom at the expense of their conscience or damage to the cause. He had indicated the pseudo-existence of idols, but he knew that it would remain a problem for the Corinthians and that they should avoid idolatry.

I Corinthians 9:1-11

The discussion in chapters 9 and 10 is probably the direct result of some of the questions asked in the letter from the church. Perhaps there were those who made the claim that Paul imposed upon the communities, much like a recent "Elmer Gantry" kind of representative. He went to great lengths to show that while as a minister he had a right to and for support, he had not made use of that right. It would appear that Paul protected himself and the missionary task from this charge by working in the tent-making trade whenever possible. This section, however, is still an effort to get them to understand how damaging the idol situation could be.

As he continued to discuss the dangers of sharing in eating portions of meats sacrificed to idols, Paul's main emphasis was on the consciences of those who felt strongly about the issue. In one sense, those people were weak, but that did not excuse anyone from respecting their positions. It was an effort to maintain the position that idols were and are meaningless, and at the same time to show that participating in idol worship, even by eating those meats, is in one sense support of the system. It is a tedious and difficult thing to deal with, and the principle has to be dealt with, even in the modern world. It is not only vitally important to the Christian cause to care deeply for the conscience of another, it is imperative.

The recognition that "all things are lawful" did not and does not mean that one can do anything one pleases. All things do not build up, and they may not be beneficial. Paul's best advice was to eat whatever is sold in the marketplace, or perhaps served in someone's home, without question. But if one is made aware that this meat had been offered in idol worship, one should avoid the meat because of another's conscience. Everything was to be done in the hopes that no offense would be given and that all would glorify God. The parting thought in the section demonstrates that Paul was not only willing to give advice but that he was also a role model. It perhaps translates to the modern community in a way that causes believers to sense the terrible, and at the same time glorious, burden of influence.

I Corinthians 11:2-14:40

This entire section deals with disorders in public worship. It is true that few are able to rise above the culture of their own time, and Paul must be seen in that light. The patriarchal domination of men over women has often colored the relationship between the sexes. In the east, the veil shows the inferior status of females, but it is also her protection.

"We must remember the status of women in Jewish eyes. Under Jewish law a woman was vastly inferior to man. According to the narrative She had been created out of Adam's rib (Genesis 2:22, 23) to be the helpmeet of man. There was a bit of fanciful rabbinic exegesis which said, 'God did not form woman out of the head, lest she should become proud; nor out of the eye, lest she should lust; nor out of the mouth, lest she should become talkative; nor out of the heart, lest she should become jealous; nor out of the hand, lest she should become covetous; nor out of the foot, lest she should become a wandering busy body; but out of a rib which was always covered; therefore, modesty should be her primary quality.'"[1]

But it was not just Paul's background that prompted his statement that women should not pray or prophesy, which meant "preach" or "proclaim," with their heads uncovered. Obviously, in this passage there is no prohibition against women speaking. According to Paul's understanding of the custom, however, it was a disgrace for a woman's head to be uncovered or for it to be shaved. (This can also be seen in the conception of how a woman should dress in the Islamic world.) It must be rabbinic training that led him to these statements in the first part of Chapter 11, but even before he had finished with the discussion, he came back to proclaim the essential partnership of man and woman. We must try to extract a principle from this section. In a situation like Corinth, it would be far better to err on the side of caution than on the side of laxness. The issue of long hair for women and short hair for men may have been a part of the culture of the time, but it really had nothing to do with spiritual value or growth.

I Corinthians 11:17-34

The discussion of the major issues of chaos and abuse in worship began to be dealt within the seventeenth verse of Chapter 11. The passage before us and the following ones are the nearest view of the worship process of the first-century church. From what is stated in this portion, it would appear that the factions alluded to in the first part of this letter disturbed the worship process. One can never be certain about when or where the *agapé* feast began, but it sounds as though it may have been where a part of the Corinthian problem was located. For slaves or the poor, the feast may have been one of the few times they received a good meal, but in Corinth, people were eating in little cliques, and while some were gorging themselves, others were going hungry. Paul also suggests that some

Idolatry and Related Problems

of them were getting drunk during those feasts. Obviously, cliquishness was a corruption of the fellowship, and he rebuked them. When he began the discussion of the Lord's Supper, he indicated that the bread represented the body of Christ which was given (sacrificed) for them. (A few of the ancient manuscripts say, "broken for you," but the better ones simply say, "This is my body which is for you.") He also used the cup as representative of the new covenant. Some have difficulty with the elements being symbols, but it must be remembered that a proper understanding of the term "symbol" from a religious point of view is vitally important, for it stands for something else, and in a unique way it participates in that for which it stands. In this discussion, there is no sense in which the elements are "mere" symbols and, therefore, lose some of their awesomeness. Whatever their understanding, it is evident that the supper was being abused, which was unacceptable. If what had already been said about people eating in little cliques and not caring about the hungry is correct, they had already denied the unity of the body, and so to come together afterwards and pretend a fellowship while partaking of the supper makes it a sin. Paul saw it that way. It must also be noted that the passage in verse 27 used the adverb "unworthily," meaning, as the NRSV translates it, "in an unworthy manner." People have been known to say that they did not participate in the communion because they were unworthy (taking it as an adjective), but that is not what is being stated in this passage. No one can ever claim to be worthy of Christ's self-surrender. What is denounced here is observing communion with the wrong attitude, either irreverently or by not paying attention to what it means. Here it is pretending that there was fellowship when there was none.

Once, when I was ministering in a church in Kentucky and was presiding over the observance of the Lord's Supper, I suddenly became impressed about something of which I had been aware for some time, but for some reason I had not connected it with this part of our worship. It was a perfect example of pretending that we had fellowship, when in reality ours had been fractured. Two of our men, who had been bosom friends for years, had a falling out. They had worked together on each other's crops, and their families had been almost inseparable. The two men even sat together in worship services, and their wives sat across the sanctuary. Fred's wife had died suddenly, and Ruby and Hayes took Fred in and often invited him to eat with them. Then whatever happened to separate them occurred. Now, when Fred came into the church building, he looked around to see where Hayes was and then went to the other side. That happened in reverse if Fred got there first. As I looked out on that miserable situation, I rashly decided that I had to try to do something about it. It was a large country church, and after a service ended most people stood around and talked almost as long as the service had lasted. That morning, when the service was over, Fred went out and stood on one side of the church yard, and Hayes went to the other side. With great fear, I went to Fred and said, "I don't know what happened between you and Hayes or what he did, and I really don't want to know, but won't you come with me and shake hands with Hayes and get past this thing?" He replied, "What he did was so bad that I could never go to him. No, I will not do that." Almost giving up, I turned and went to the other man. His father had been a minister, and I thought I could fudge a little and appeal to him through that. So I said, "Hayes, I have asked Fred to come over here and speak to you, but he won't do that. You know that your father would want you to settle this, so won't you be first and go with me over to Fred and hold out your hand to him?" He looked at me, I thought almost with scorn, and said, "What he did to me was terrible and I can't do that, but if he will hold out his hand, I will shake it." I thought, what am I dealing with, two eight-year-olds? Then I went back to Fred, and I admit this was sneaky, but I said, "Fred, you have a chance to be the bigger man here. Hayes has said that if you would come over there and hold out your hand, he would shake hands with you." All the while I had Fred by the arm and was nudging him toward the other side. I don't know whether he caught what was happening or not, but when those two guys got close, they threw their arms around each other and wept like babies. The fellowship was restored. I never found out what had happened between them and I somehow doubt that they knew, but Fred went home with Ruby and Hayes for lunch.

Communion cannot be observed properly with unforgiven ruptures in the fellowship. It cannot be observed properly without remembering and understanding what Jesus did for us. It is sometimes called the "Eucharist," which has to do with gratitude. It never means that everyone has to agree on everything, theologically or otherwise, but it does mean that cliques, barriers to fellowship, and bitterness must be overcome if the supper is to carry its significance. The last portion of Paul's admonition did not mean that it was wrong to observe the love feast and communion, but it did mean that divisiveness and cliquishness should never be allowed to destroy the unity of fellowship.

I Corinthians 12:1-30

The Exercise of Spiritual Gifts:

There must have been many issues regarding the way worship was being carried out. The apostles were held in a high position of honor, but beyond them, one needs always to remember that there was no formal clergy at this time. Anyone could prophesy (better translated as "preach"). Anyone could say whatever he/she felt was important, perhaps like a Quaker service, and all gifts were seen by Paul as under the leadership of the Spirit. But the free atmosphere must have opened the door to chaotic hours in which intelligent instruction could not prevail. As has been mentioned earlier, there must have been those in the missionary party who functioned in the capacity of *hyperetes*, or instructor, especially since the new converts had no way of knowing the message of the church concerning the life and teachings of Jesus except by oral transmission. There were no gospels, nor do there seem to have been any written instructions to leave behind, so when Silas or Timothy or any other knowledgeable leader left, the new community may have been somewhat at a loss. It is correct that Paul stayed at Corinth for at least a year and a half, and that Priscilla and Aquila appear to have been instructors. But even with all of that, when Paul left this group, Priscilla and Aquila went to Ephesus, and we have no way of following Silas and Timothy. It is probable that few were qualified to lead the church. Usually the church met in small groups (house churches), and there does not seem to have been a planned order of service. As a result, anyone could have felt an urge to speak, which may have led to part of the confusion we confront in this letter.

This section begins by attempting to show that there is a unity to be preserved even though there are varying gifts. Paul tried by illustration to show that all of these were from one Spirit, and that the church should function as a body with one purpose. He illustrated the use of various gifts by likening them to different parts of the body (foot, hand, eye, and ear) and by showing that they contribute to the welfare of the total body in their particular ways. No one gift is more important than any other and none operates by itself, but each contributes to the health of the whole. So it is with spiritual gifts and abilities. But even the various gifts were to be brought together and subordinated to the whole.

Since the major issue regarding spiritual gifts is the dominant theme of Chapter 12 and continued in Chapter 14, it is interesting that Paul inserted the beautiful poem regarding *agapé*, probably as the only thing that could correct all of the issues.

I Corinthians 13:1-13

The greatest gift of all:

It is not possible to do justice to the great prose-poem; it speaks for itself. Some have suggested that this poem is the greatest of all of Paul's writings, and the idea has been expressed that the passage is so exalted that Paul may have composed it separately, polished it carefully, and then selected it for use here because it put to rest completely the arguments in Corinth about the use of spiritual gifts, especially chaotic tongues.[2]

This discussion interrupts the argument of the letter and demonstrates beautifully that egotistic and arrogant use of any gift is worth nothing. This is another place where one would like to know how the cliques in Corinth contributed to or prided themselves in the use of showy gifts. Perhaps there was information in the questions submitted to Paul; we cannot know.

The proposal "If I speak" is a conditional sentence that grammarians call a third class condition. It states an unfulfilled condition and probably means, "Even if I speak with fantastic utterances, I may or may not, but if I do it is worthless unless it is done with *agapé*."[3] It is this characteristic quality that Paul describes both negatively and positively. The word *agapé* was rarely used until the Septuagint and New Testament writers appropriated it. Perhaps its rarity made it special, but Christian writers "baptized" the term so that it has a refined meaning. It is used to describe the love that is inherent in the nature of God. It represents a part of the impact of the life of Jesus as contrasted with the other Greek terms for love. Each of the other words implies that I love someone because there is something that attracts me and creates a situation in which I can gain something for myself from the object loved. It may be sexual, or what I can gain from a friendship, or even the security or aid that I can gain from my family. But God's love is not emotional; it is not dependent on the object loved, but on the giving nature of the one loving. It is concerned only for what can be done for the well-being of the one loved.

Instead of power, gain, control, manipulation, and coercion by which the forces of the world (and, sadly, sometimes the humans in the church) have constantly attempted to rule, the new values lie in the qualities Paul sees in *agapé*. All gifts are valueless if they stem from any other motive than from *agapé*. A community can do without some gifts, but without *agapé* it will die.[4] So no gifts with which he will deal (ecstatic speaking, prophecy/preaching, knowledge, or even that which is termed "faith") will have any significance without *agapé*. One might even be able to understand angelic communications (probably a rabbinic concept of a special worship language) and have any or all gifts, but without *agapé* they are useless.[5]

Paul began this tribute to love by contrasting *agapé* with all other religious activities. Considering how this interrupts the discussion about disorders in public worship, it almost appears that he was saying, "Go on doing your self-elevating expressions, boasting about how gifted you are, and exalting yourselves over others. It is totally empty noise when it is not transformed by *agapé*." Then he characterized the better and most excellent way. The *agapé* quality of love is always patient, gracious, and kind. Although he characterizes it negatively, each of those characterizations underscores that it is not egotistical, self-promoting, or arrogantly self-seeking. One obvious issue throughout human history has been the desire of people to "jump on" someone when something bad occurs. Paul stated that *agapé* love never enjoys the bad, but enjoys the good. In some sense that may reinforce the idea that *agapé* covers a multitude of sins and protects with confident trust. It is *agapé* that is the ultimate survivor because, as John (I John 2:4) put it, "God is *agapé*." Everything else appears to be both temporary and imperfect, and if there were to be a solution to the problems regarding the disorders in public worship, the diversity of gifts or any other issue, it would come through the exercise of the better way: *love*.

I Corinthians 14:1-25

Chaos in worship services:

After the great interlude of advice on love, Paul returned to the problem of chaos in worship, caused primarily by those who spoke unintelligibly. It should be easy to determine that what was happening in Corinth was not the same as that which occurred on the Day of Pentecost, when people had heard and understood the message. (At various times in the history of the church, things which may have not been clearly stated have been interpreted by people in ways different from what originally was meant or happened.) These tongues were not understood by the group and therefore, if they were valid expressions at all, they could only be expressions to God. Perhaps this was like a prayer language or a crying out when words could not be found to express the thoughts involved. It must have created a disorderly situation, for Paul suggested that an outsider who came by would consider the group out of their minds. His conclusion was that there should be order even in the use of tongues, and not only should they wait and speak in turn, but no tongue should be used unless it could be interpreted. The instruction seems to conform to the rest of the letter, in that all things should be done for the building up of the body. Paul did not disparage such speech; instead, he stated that even though he *could* speak in tongues, in the assembly he would rather speak five meaningful (intelligent) words than speak 10,000 in unintelligible gibberish. One can sense that an idea had emerged that those who spoke in tongues were superior Christians to those who did not, which contributed to a spirit of arrogance.

Paul used a rabbinic argument. One must never forget that he was a trained rabbi, and his training often showed in his arguments. Reaching back to a passage in Isaiah (28:11-12), he showed that even Israel was instructed by people of strange languages which they either did not understand or did not heed. Likewise, those outsiders who might hear but not understand would be turned off and not respond. Therefore, while tongues might be a sign for believers, outsiders would not understand, just as Israel had not. But intelligible preaching is an understandable sign for believers, and outsiders may come to believe because they observe meaningful worship. (Verses 21-25 are difficult to follow, and their interpretation by scholars varies.)

I Corinthians 14: 26-40

The entire thrust of this section is that a worship service should be orderly and meaningful to all; tongues should be limited (to two or three) and not run amok. None should be used in worship if no one is able to interpret what the tongue means. It would appear that tongues were an intensely emotional experience, and to limit emotion in this way would almost stifle its expression. Even preaching (prophecy) should be done in an orderly manner and with limitations, for "God is not a God of disorder, but of peace."

A number of scholars believe that verses 34-36 were not a part of the original letter, but were added to return to the old patriarchal ideas, even though there is no textual evidence for this theory. The idea does have some merit, because Paul had talked about women having the gift of prophecy, so how could he turn so completely and forbid them to speak? Still others have suggested that this might refer to a problem that could occur if women sat in the rear, as they did in the synagogues, or maybe in another room in house churches; if someone were trying to make a copy of the letter as it was being read (which probably occurred quite often) and something was said that the women did not understand, they could have produced some confusion by asking each other what was said. If that should be the case, the reader may have told them to wait until they got home and ask their husbands, who had probably heard clearly. So if a copy were being made and if the reader simply said for the women to be quiet, the words about keeping silent could have been put in the copy by the scribe, and when it got to another church the restriction was preserved in future manuscripts. The passage does seem to make women second-class church members, and in the light of what Paul wrote in Galatians 3:28 — "in Christ there is no longer Jew nor Greek, slave, nor free, there is no longer male nor female" — second-class Christian citizenship is not permissible. Since there were various prophetesses, it is difficult to make this restriction consistent.[6]

Idolatry and Related Problems

Issues related to the resurrection:

The basic Christian concept relating to life after death depends on the resurrection of Jesus. While there were those who argued both pro and con about the possibility of life after death (which had been discussed long before the time of Jesus), the actual story of the resurrection of Christ was the benchmark on which the entire message depended. If Jesus had not been raised from the dead, it is doubtful that the good news would have gotten off the ground. Certainly, it could have been no more than another philosophy about life, and the Christian reversal of so many things the world had leaned on would have made it difficult to sustain. The world had, from the beginning of human history, depended on military control over others as the force that moved and ordered society; it depended on greed (and still does) as a root desire for controlling the economy; it used humans as animals; slavery was a dominant force. To imagine a society dominated by love, peace, kindness, understanding, selflessness, and many other virtues that Christian followers have adopted, if only partially, would have been unthinkable. (No wonder Frederik Nietzsche believed that Jesus had turned the world upside down.) One of the qualifications for replacing Judas was that the replacement must have witnessed the resurrection, and a part of the *kerygma* had always dealt with the resurrection for support since it had depended on those who were eyewitnesses to the risen Lord. The first part of Chapter 15 deals with a number of witnesses who had seen the risen Jesus, and the unique appearance to Paul was the last one he mentioned. Any assessment of the validity of those claims depends on the trust one has in the integrity of those first-century followers. No argument can be offered to sustain their testimony from a demonstrable, materialistic point of view, but it would take a greater acting job than most can imagine to transform that fearful little band of followers into the bold witnesses who confronted both the responsible Jewish leadership and the Roman authorities.

I Corinthians 15:12-34

It is not surprising that there should be questions about life after death, and we know that there were those in the area of Corinth who would have denied that there was any such thing as life after death, even as there are in the present age. So the entire proclamation and validity of faith hinge on the resurrection of Christ. Paul's instructions regarding the doubts or questions of the Corinthians focus on Jesus' resurrection. Paul used the first-century idea of a culmination of history and God's ultimate victory over death to support his claim. There is a bit of difficulty in Paul's thinking, for at some points he looks forward to the Jewish concept of a final "day of judgment," and at other times he writes as if when one dies, he/she goes immediately to be with the Lord (II Corinthians 5:6-9). This remains an unsolved issue, but the majority of Christians have taken the stance that entrance into the presence of the Lord occurs immediately at the point of a believer's death. It can be supported by the experience of the repentant thief when Jesus said, "This day you shall be with me in paradise." This would obviously mean that the phrase that implied a "day of judgment" would refer to a long undetermined period continuing as long as earthly history lasts, rather than to a single day of culmination.

There must also have been a custom involving baptism by proxy. (Paul did not discuss whether this had any validity or not.) Such a concept would never have been thought of if there were no resurrection. It is simple logic that if there is no afterlife or accounting of what one has been, the only philosophy that makes sense is that of extreme Epicureanism, and it is foolish for one to sacrifice and work for "good," since the only known value is immediate pleasure.

II Corinthians 15:35-38

The question from the church had apparently dealt with the nature of eternity. Paul's answer was illustrated by the process of planting and reaping, and it led to his concept of a "spiritual body." Whatever that "body" may be like no one can have a hint, unless he/she takes as fact the statements of those who have had what is called a "near death" experience or suggests that it lies in the appearances of the "peculiar body" of the risen Lord. (It should be noted that "near death" experiences are just that, *near* death, and that many of them explain the eternal sphere in terms of what they are used to in this realm.) All of this shows how difficult it is for humans to even try to think spiritually, for we have no language except that of symbols. For Paul, it seems to imply that the spiritual realm is the ultimate reality and does not involve flesh and blood, i.e. the physical/material. This will be difficult for many to think about, for the only way we can visualize (which is also a physical term) those who are deceased is to recall in memory their physical appearances. However, the eternal realm is one where death is eliminated with all of its sorrows, so believers can be encouraged because of the victory of God in Christ. The same issue was seen in Thessalonica when believers began to die. What does eternal life mean if people are dying? Their world view of heaven above and Gehenna below must have affected the possibilities they saw. Since that materialistic view has been discarded, the existence of the spiritual realm and its permanent reality must be the victorious answer. One thing was certain for Paul: Whatever life after death is, it retains personal identity.

The two ideas — one dealing with a kind of suspended animation at death, with its day of judgment at the conclusion, and the opposing idea that judgment occurs for each individual at the point of physical death — have existed side by side throughout theological history.

The dominant current view is probably the latter, but there are still those who hold to the first-century world view and its concept of time, largely because we are hard-pressed to find the tools to think spiritually and can only do so through symbols. In either case, the Corinthians were told that the ultimate victory came through God's action in the experience of Jesus, which means that nothing done in the service of Jesus and in the correct spirit can ever be futile. The objection that the judgment of a person can never be made until his/her influence runs its course is a matter of works and a tally sheet of one's good and bad points. But if one's judgment is based on his/her character likeness to Christ, that is certainly determined at the point when one exits this physical life. Obviously, it is a matter of faith.

The remainder of the letter deals with hopes of a future visit and the unity of Paul's work with that of others. Attempting to solve the issues took much tedious labor and concern (and perhaps some of those have not and perhaps cannot be completely solved), but ultimately the obstacles (mountains) were overcome and the gospel moved on.

---

[1]William Barclay, *The Letters to the Corinthians*, rev. ed. (Philadelphia: Westminster Press,1976), 98.

[2]C. K. Barrett, *The First Epistle to the Corinthians* (New York: Harper and Row Publishers, 1968), 299ff.

[3]Archibald T. Robertson, *Word Pictures in the New Testament*, vol. IV (New York: Harper and Brothers Publishers, 1931), 176.

[4]F.F. Bruce, *New Century Bible Commentary, I and II Corinthians* (Grand Rapids: W. B. Eerdman's Publishers, 1980), 124.

[5]Barclay, 117.

[6]*Harper and Collins Study Bible* (London: Harper and Collins Publishers, 1989), footnote 14:34-36, 2160.

Chapter 24

The Journey Comes to Its Conclusion

The problems at Corinth had occupied much of Paul's time and energy while he was at Ephesus. Shortly before he returned to Jerusalem for what turned out to be the last time, he had sent Timothy and Erastus to Macedonia. During this last period of Paul's work in Ephesus, a riot erupted. So much is not told regarding the problems at Ephesus that to attempt a reconstruction of his experiences there would be problematical. It would appear that at some point he was imprisoned, and he even described it in the Corinthian letter (I Corinthians 15:32) as "having fought with the wild beasts." We have no information about it, and we must remain uncertain whether he was actually thrown into the arena with wild animals or whether the statement is metaphorical, since it was highly unlikely that a Roman citizen would be put in that situation. He alluded to many trials, and often we have little information regarding those experiences. But Luke was not offering a chronicle of Paul's life; he was showing the progress of the gospel in spite of obstacles. It does appear that while the little community may not have had conflicts with the Ephesian synagogue earlier, after Paul came on the scene there was a rupture that also manifested itself in economic conflicts.

The city of Ephesus was one of the major cities in the province. It was where the supreme Roman authority, the proconsul, administered justice on "court days," which were probably held about three times a month. The opposition raised against Paul was purely economic. There is no indication of any great theological difficulty, since there were often philosophers and others who opposed idolatry.[1] The worship of Artemis was centered in Ephesus with a great temple which has been excavated during the last century. The image of Artemis (or the Roman Diana) was said to have fallen from the sky. In terms of the first-century world view, that would have been heaven. (One cannot help but see the parallels with the Kaaba stone of Islam and the book of Mormon, which is said to have fallen from heaven into the yard of Joseph Smith.) It must have been a meteorite, and the representations of her having her upper body covered with breasts must have linked her with fertility worship. Some indicate that the image at Ephesus may have been carved from a block of wood, and it was so ancient that it was described as having fallen from heaven so long ago that no one really knew where it had come from. However that reputation was gained, Ephesus became known as the "temple keeper" of Artemis, and the marvelous temple was a significant economic boom to the city. The temple was one of the wonders of the ancient world. Demetrius seems to have been one of the prime movers of the guild of silversmiths, and his main pitch was that their wealth, which was probably significant, was at stake. He believed it necessary to stop Paul since, apparently, inroads had been made into the business of making images of Artemis and silver replicas of the temple. Why a Jew, named Alexander, was forced to the forefront is not clear, but he had absolutely no success in quelling the riot. There is good reason to believe that The Way had achieved a pretty good foothold in Asia, and the evidence of many churches (cf. the Apocalypse and some of the letters of Paul to churches) indicates some thriving Christian communities. Paul's traveling companions, Gaius and Aristarchus, were seized, and although Paul apparently felt obligated to go to their defense, his friends prevented him. Knowing how mob psychology works, it may be assumed that if he had gotten into the crowd, serious harm could have come to him. The wisdom of the town clerk and the threat that Rome might take away their independence and the position of the city quieted the mob.

Acts 20:1-6

It is worth noting that Paul left Ephesus soon after this event and returned to Greece for about three months. He seems to have planned to leave from Greece, perhaps from Cenchrea, and go to Syria, but when a Jewish plot against him was discovered, he changed his mind and went through Macedonia. He sent seven workers ahead to Troas. There they waited for the rest of the party, which must now have included Luke, since he again began to use the personal pronoun "we." The journey began just after the spring season, and Paul appears to have hoped to be in Jerusalem for Pentecost.

Acts 20:7-16

There is much that is not covered in this short passage. The decision to go overland through Macedonia, instead of sailing from Cenchrea, led Paul through Philippi and then on to Troas. He must have at least suspected that this would be the last time he would visit Troas, for he indicated that he intended to go to Rome, apparently for another phase of his work. It would be normal to attempt to give them all of the instruction that he could on this last visit. The description of the service leaves the reader with a little uncertainty as to when it occurred. The "first day of the week" would have been on Sunday, if Luke used the Roman calculation about when the day began, but if he used the Jewish method, the day would have begun at dusk on Saturday. It makes little difference except that, using Roman calculations, the early church, dominated by Gentiles, had already begun to use Sunday as the "Lord's Day" and shifted its worship to that time. However, the statements in Luke's account imply that the meeting was held at night and that the room was hot, since there would have been many oil lamps burning and the service would have lasted for a long time. There was an exciting event, which had no bearing on the content of the service, but made an impression on the group only because of the nature of the interruption. A young man named Eutychus went to sleep while sitting in a window. As Luke put it, Eutychus fell three stories and was thought to be dead. Some scholars believe that Luke included this account to place Paul on the level of Peter in the raising of Dorcas, Elijah, Elisha, and even the Lord.[2] There are others who suggest that with the inclusion of verse 10, the report may mean that Eutychus was simply unconscious. Since the text permits either interpretation, the issue will probably not be settled with certainty.[3] Of course, such a startling event would have upset people, and even though Paul indicated that Eutychus was still alive, resumption of the service would have been difficult. Yet after eating something, Paul continued his instruction and spoke all night. The people were joyous on Eutychus' return about daybreak. The party left Troas, and the narrative simply gives an eyewitness report of the islands they touched until they came to Miletus. (No reason was even hinted as to why Paul went overland from Troas to Assos.) This is more evidence that Paul never renounced his Jewish heritage, for he avoided going into Ephesus so that he could be in Jerusalem for the Feast of Pentecost. He could not bypass the people of Ephesus completely, but there were too many dangers that might delay him. So he did not risk a visit into the city, but had the church leaders meet him in Miletus.

Acts 20:17-38

Although it is never said, there are many who believe that the ship for this part of the voyage was chartered. Paul was carrying an offering for the aid of the Jerusalem Christians, and the group with him was rather large. He seemed to be in charge of where the ship would stop and how long it would stay in port.

"The mention of 'the ship' in verses thirteen and thirty-eight contrasted with 'a ship' in 22:2 and the fact that they were coasting along, stopping (for longer than a night) only where Paul wished, viz. at Miletus, would almost indicate that they had chartered a coasting vessel in Troas or even at Philippi, to take them as far as Lycia. They were not a small party and they were also in a hurry and it would have been difficult to find a coasting vessel which did not stop at Ephesus."[4]

Paul did feel the need to talk with the leaders of the church and so he had them meet him at Miletus. It was a farewell speech, for Paul was convinced that he would not see them again. In the speech, he defended his character and showed that he had not taken anything from them, but worked at his own trade so as not to be a burden or give any cause for criticism. It has already been said that during his stay at Ephesus he had gone through a difficult time, especially with the issues at Corinth, in which his leadership and motives had been questioned. It also seems that the Christians lived in a rather peaceful way with the synagogue until Paul came, after which there was a rather sharp division. Notice the reference to "fierce wolves" who would attempt to destroy the group (20:29-30). In his final speech, Paul emphasized the necessity for unity between the Gentile Christians and the Jewish ones. In a later letter, which most scholars believe was a circular one to the churches in Asia, Paul emphasized the importance of breaking down the "dividing wall," (Ephesians 2:14-22) and creating or strengthening their unity. The gathering and taking of an offering for the relief of the Jerusalem community would appear to be the reason Paul felt the need and the urgency to go to Jerusalem. It was a dangerous place for him, and many tried to stop him from going. There is a touching scene at the point when they said "goodbye" to him, and it indicates that there were many who felt deep emotional ties to him and probably great fear for him.

Acts 21:1-16

There is no need to recount the journey Paul and his party made from Lycia to Phoenicia, a seven-day trip. It appears that the chartered ship did not go farther than Lycia, and that they found passage on commercial ships from that point on. It is extremely interesting that everywhere Paul stopped, the people feared for his life. There was a strong belief that the Spirit was leading in the direction that Paul not go to Jerusalem. But Paul disagreed. Again, there is a pointed statement about Philip's daughters serving as prophetesses. In light of other discussions about Paul's attitude toward women participating in worship, it is fairly evident that to avoid the perception that there were both prophetesses and deaconesses in the early churches, the only alternative is to pick and choose which passages one wants to follow or imply a meaning to the languages as they were written. It is also obvious, with the object lesson from Agabas and the urging of the people, that they were absolutely convinced that the Spirit was leading strongly that Paul not visit Jerusalem, but he was just as convinced that he should. With his declaration that he was prepared even to die if necessary, they stopped their efforts and in a rather unusual statement said, "The will of the Lord be done." This seems to have been a statement of resignation, and since they could not convince Paul that their understanding of the Spirit's leading was correct, they deferred to him.

[1] Rackham, *The Acts of the Apostles*, 363ff.
[2] Rackham, 380-381.
[3] Stagg, *The Book of Acts*, 210, 211.
[4] Rackham, Ibid.

Chapter 25

The Return to Jerusalem

Acts 21:17-26

The return to Jerusalem was just as had been expected by many of the people who warned Paul not to go there. The members of the church, especially James and the leaders, seemed pleased to see Paul and to hear of the things that had happened since they last saw him. We do not know whether there had been any communication during those travels, but now they hear of a great Gentile ministry. Many in the church at Jerusalem had not been particularly sympathetic to what had been done under Paul's leadership, and even though the letter had been adopted and sent, there was always an undercurrent of dissatisfaction and opposition to what he had done. The leaders seemed to believe that such a letter was not only for those in Galatia, but also for all Gentiles who had become or would become believers. Those leaders of the Jerusalem community, even though they apparently believed that the Gentile missions were in harmony with the guidance of God, were in a bit of a theological bind. Much of the Jerusalem community was earnestly concerned that their Jewish heritage was eroding, largely under Paul's leadership. They were still Jews, and they were concerned about maintaining Jewish influence in the advance of the Christiana movement. The mountain had been breached, but it was still there. It almost appears that there was still a danger of the development of both a Jewish church and a Gentile church, with different understandings of the purpose and value of the law. This perplexity is seen in verse 22 in the question, "What is to be done?" It would be a mistake to conclude that the Jerusalem Conference satisfied the various elements in the church and put the matter to rest. The rumor that Paul was teaching against the law and that the Gentile, Trophimus, was in the temple, was spread, most likely inaccurately, and it may have been a mistake or even a deliberate falsehood. As most remember, there was a Court of the Gentiles in the temple, and any person, Jew or Gentile, could go there. Beyond that was the Court of Israel, where no Gentile was allowed. Trophimus had a perfect right to be in the Court of the Gentiles, so seeing him in the city with Paul and assuming that he had gone beyond that area, someone developed the story. It is absolutely absurd to think that Paul deliberately dared to commit that infraction.

It is correct that the ultimate outcome of the gospel of grace would involve setting aside Jewish regulations, and that may be what was of vital concern to the Jewish members of the Jerusalem church. Paul had often said that Gentiles were not required to keep the Jewish law, but we have no record of him ever saying the same about Jewish Christians. Since we do not know anything about what was said in those arguments with the various groups in Asia, it may have easily been interpreted the way the rumor implies. Some of the source of the rumor may have come from some Jews from the Diaspora who had argued with Paul in those synagogue experiences. But once before, at the conclusion of the "second" journey, Paul had made a vow himself, shaved his head, and most likely brought the hair back to be offered in the temple. So in the current situation there was only one way to hope to counter the rumor, and that was, in some way, to show that Paul was still a good practicing Jew. One way to do so was to have him participate in a Jewish ceremony of a vow, probably paying a portion of the expenses, and going through the rites of Jewish purification. (It would be difficult to prove that a person did not believe in prayer if one observed that person praying.)

James and the elders stated firmly that what they were asking of him did not affect the Gentiles. Even though the Jerusalem church had sent the letter, many of them may not have believed that the gospel of faith alone was sufficient, and certainly not for the Jewish believers. So their zeal for the Jewish law would at some point conflict with the Gentile missions. Paul acquiesced and was willing to bear the expenses for the four men.

> "This is the law for the Nazarites when the time for their consecration has been completed: they shall be brought to the entrance of the tent of meeting, and they shall offer their gift to the Lord, one male lamb without blemish, as a burnt offering, one ram without blemish as an offering of well-being, and a basket of unleavened bread, cakes of choice flour mixed with oil, and unleavened wafers spread with oil, with their grain offerings and their drink offerings." Numbers 16:13-15

But when the purification period had almost been completed, some Jews, who must have known Paul and who probably opposed him in Asia, stirred up the people after they had seen him in the temple. They either honestly assumed that since Paul had a Greek, Trophimus, with him in the city, he had taken him into the temple, or else they deliberately used that rumor to stir up the people, and another riot occurred. They apparently dragged Paul into the Court of the Gentiles and mobbed him. He was arrested in the temple.

Acts 21:27-36

The focus of this section is to bring the ministry of Paul to a conclusion with the conflicts relating to Jewish legalism versus the gospel of grace and freedom that he proclaimed. As can easily be seen, friends of Paul all along the way, perhaps more aware of the climate in Jerusalem, warned of this climactic clash. It is necessary to read not only what is said, but what is not said.

James, the brother of Jesus, had become the respected leader of the Jerusalem church. The church was saturated and anchored in the Jewish legal tradition, and even though certain concessions had been made to the Gentiles, there does not seem to have been much progress theologically among those Christians. It was a church that interpreted the gospel in legalistic terms and, according to James' statement, myriads of believers were very zealous for the law. It is not possible to know the intensity of the antagonism of the Hebrew Christians to the message of Paul, but there is ample reason to believe that it was violent and that the issues had not been solved. Neither should one hide piously behind the idea that there were no Christians in the various mobs or suggest that the problems were with the non-Christian Jews, although there are commentators who believe that those who instigated the accusations were only Asian non-Christian Jews.[1] Throughout the history of religions, the pious have often done atrocious things in the name of God. This was a violent antagonism, and it seems to have incorporated a systematic representation of Paul's teaching and behavior.[2] James' suggestion about what Paul should do was a concession to that wing of the church, but as long as it did not compromise the basic principle of grace, it posed no problem for Paul. In fact, on the last previous occasion when he was in Jerusalem, Paul had consummated a Jewish vow. It must be repeated that Paul never renounced his Jewish heritage, but while he could involve himself in observations such as these, he also never compromised his "gospel." If the narrative tells us the entire story, James and the Jerusalem church never seem to have come to the defense of Paul, but rather tried to avoid conflict. Paul came prepared to try to bridge the gap between the two wings of the church, but to satisfy those who knew dogmatically that their position was the correct one was a monstrous task. It would appear, however, that Paul knew which battles to fight, and since this suggestion represented no compromise of principle, he willingly participated.

Even though we have previously looked at part of the design of the temple, one cannot read this narrative and absorb its full impact without reconstructing the attitudes about the layout of the temple. The area was a large enclosure, most of which was open-air. Upon entering the temple, one's first encounter was with the Court of the Gentiles. Beyond that was a partition with gates beyond which only Jews could go. An inscription over the gates indicated that any foreigner who ventured beyond the gates did so on the pain of death.[3]

> "One of these inscriptions was discovered by Clermont-Ganneau in 1871 the stone on which the eyes of Jesus and St. Paul may have rested is now in the Imperial New Museum at Constantinople. The inscription is as follows: Let no foreigner enter within the screen and enclosure surrounding the sanctuary."[4]

Beyond that lay the Court of Israel, which was for men only, and beyond that was the Court of the Priests. The temple building proper housed the Holy Place, and a tremendous veil divided it from the Holy of Holies.

Paul had a perfect right to be inside the wall, where he apparently was first accosted with the accusation that he had brought a Gentile into the temple. As has been mentioned, Luke indicated that they did this because they had seen him in the city with Trophimus, who was a Greek, and they made the assumption that he had violated the temple. (It would strain one's imagination to the breaking point to think that Paul, who certainly knew of this prohibition, would have deliberately violated it when he had gone to such lengths to prove that he was a good Jew.) It must be assumed that Paul was at least in the Court of the Women and perhaps in the Court of Israel, where only Jewish men could go. The actions of the mob defy all logic. All that it took to stir up the crowd was an accusation that Paul had done exactly what the rumor had said. So they dragged him outside the Court of Israel, probably to the Court of the Gentiles, and proceeded to assault him with the intention of killing him. Some may wonder how this could take place. The Romans often allowed the Jews to take care of their own law problems. However, since they were probably in the outer part of the temple, the Romans could intervene and try to quell the riot. Paul was rescued by the Romans, and as the tribune tried to find out what had caused the riot, they found it necessary to forcibly remove Paul from the scene. He was probably taken to the Tower of Antonia, where the troops were stationed. The crowd cried, "Away with him."

Acts 21:37-22:2

Paul attempts a defense

If we can trust Josephus, this must have been a chaotic time in Judea. Bands of robbers plagued the area, and many of them sought to bring about a rebellion against Rome. The issue to which the tribune referred was likely an effort by one who was probably a Zealot who came from Egypt and persuaded a large group to follow him by promising as a prophet that he would make the walls of Jerusalem fall down, gain access to the city, and take it back from Roman control. Judea must have been a difficult place to administer, for this was not the only uprising. Felix, the procurator, had ordered a military operation against the group led by the Egyptian, and the rebellion was crushed. The Egyptian leader escaped, but 400 of his followers were killed and 200 were captured.

> "But there was an Egyptian false prophet that did the Jews more mischief than did the former; for he was a cheat and pretended to be a prophet also and got together thirty thousand men that were deluded by him; these he led around about from the wilderness to the mount which is called the Mount of Olives, and was ready to break into Jerusalem by force from that place; and if he could but once conquer the Roman garrison and the people he intended to domineer over them by the assistance of those guards of his that were to break into the city with him. But Felix prevented his attempt, and met him with his Roman soldiers while all the people assisted him in his attack upon them, insomuch that when it came to a battle, the Egyptian ran away with a few others while the greatest part of those who were with him were either destroyed or taken alive; but the rest of the multitude were dispersed to their homes, and there concealed themselves."[5]

Obviously, that leader was the object of a Roman manhunt, and the tribune thought that he had captured a prize. When Paul spoke to the tribune in Greek and asked permission to speak to the temple mob, the tribune was surprised to discover that he was not the Egyptian that he thought he had apprehended. There was little chance that Paul could convince the crowd, but he made the effort.

Acts 22:3-21

This narration of Paul's background, his early role in persecuting the church, and his personal confrontation with the risen Christ were given to show the mob that he was a good Jew and, perhaps, to diffuse the anger which they had demonstrated because of the rumor that he had defiled the temple. The Jewish people were no strangers to visions, and Paul's statement about his conversion experience would not have aroused any hostility. There is an insertion in the story, in verses 17-21, that had not been stated before. In other accounts concerning why Paul left Jerusalem, it seems to be implied that the community in Jerusalem brought about that journey, but in this one he tells of another vision in which he was told by the risen Lord to escape the danger in Jerusalem. The two accounts may not be at odds, since both could be accurate, and Paul left Jerusalem willingly. He was later in Tarsus when Barnabas went there and brought him to Antioch. None of that part of the speech produced any problem, but when he said that he understood his commission to be one that involved Gentiles, the riot erupted again. The religiously exclusive attitude of the Jews was the source of their antagonism and their desire to get rid of Paul. It is a little strange that the Jerusalem church does not seem to have tried to intervene and help Paul. Perhaps it was because the church was so heavily Jewish and had to try to continue to live in that community.

Acts 22:22-30

When the riot resumed, the tribune took further steps to get Paul away from the mob, probably more because he needed information than for Paul's protection. One of the normal ways of gaining information was through flogging, and while that may seem like torture to the modern mind, many similar methods have been used throughout history to make prisoners talk. Once before, in Philippi, Paul had resorted to his Roman citizenship for protection. There were certain rights and privileges which accrued to a citizen, and to violate such rights would have put the tribune in jeopardy. So both he and those who had bound Paul felt the danger. Paul's citizenship has been discussed before, and this account adds that he had been born into Roman citizenship. The tribune could not allow Paul to fall into the hands of the mob; his only course was to free (unbind) him and yet protect him. This was a dilemma for Claudius Lysias. He found himself forced to protect a Roman citizen, but at the same time he needed to appease the Jewish ruling body, which the Romans respected. The Sanhedrin, in a sense, often greatly aided the Roman authorities, and to have ignored them would have probably created another issue for Lysias. The mob had created the uproar, but the mob had no authority. If that uproar were the sum and substance of the antagonism against Paul, then he should have been set free. More rode on this event than just what the mob had cried out, and so it became necessary for Lysias to order a proper hearing and make some legitimate decision about Paul. So Lysias kept him in custody until the next day, when he was to stand before the Council.

Acts 23:1-10

The entire narrative, from the beginning of the temple riot through the final exit to Rome, has been studied intently by scholars. Many believe that Luke only knew the salient points and that he constructed much of the account, but the basic content is probably accurate. The exact structure of this meeting cannot be known. Some commentators contend that since Lysias had ordered the meeting and brought Paul to it, he was initially in control. This is a moot point, however, since Paul took the initiative and addressed the Sanhedrin before anyone had lodged a charge against him. Paul addressed the members of the court as equals, "brothers," and proclaimed his innocence before God. Why Ananias, the high priest from 48 until 58 C.E., commanded that Paul be struck may also remain unknown. It may have been Paul's arrogance in making a claim of innocence before the proceedings had actually begun, and therefore Ananias was in effect saying, "Shut up!" Or it may have been Paul's use of the name of God in his claim of innocence, which seemed blasphemous and therefore was subject to punishment. Whatever the reason, most interpreters see it as drawing forth an angered response on the part of Paul, perhaps because he knew how the proceeding should have been conducted and that the defendant should be treated as innocent until the verdict was announced.

His response has been seen as reflecting many different possibilities, and again, no one can ever know. When he, in a sense, pronounced a curse on the one who ordered the striking and called him a "whitewashed wall," he obviously was infuriated. But when those near him challenged him because he had spoken evil of the high priest, his response, "I did not know that he was high priest," is baffling. Several solutions have been offered:

a) The unofficial ordering of the meeting may have been so swift that the robes which were typically worn were not put on, and therefore, the identity of the high priest was unknown to the defendant, especially since he had become high priest while Paul had been away from Jerusalem.

b) Paul's alleged poor eyesight may have kept him from recognizing the high priest.

c) Some have suggested that this is a statement of irony, indicating that whoever gave the order was not acting like a high priest.

d) It may have been a simple outburst of temper.

Whatever the case, the outburst put Paul in a serious situation. If he had not known it before, it was certainly plain now; he would have a difficult time getting a fair hearing. So having already known the make-up of the Sanhedrin, he may have planned to throw in this "monkey wrench." The issue of the resurrection of the dead was clearly disruptive, and so it served a purpose in this case. Here Paul deliberately caused a division over this issue, and it gave him support from the Pharisees. This may seem a little amazing, since the primary problem had been Paul's alleged violation of the law, which should have placed the Pharisees against him. But Luke stated that the dissension became so violent that the tribune (forced to protect a Roman citizen again) rescued Paul. Whether this was a shrewd maneuver, ethical or not, will be decided by the reader.

Acts 23:11-15

Paul, like any human, needed reassurance. It came through a vision. He had long been convinced that he would go to Rome and even beyond. So with his Roman citizenship as his insurance, he could face those fanatics.

This issue was so intense for the Jews that they resorted to the most violent solution possible. One must be reminded again that throughout history, those who have been dogmatically convinced that they were right, even among Christian people, have turned to annihilation. It must also be remembered that from their point of view, the Sanhedrin had the authority to both examine and execute those who had violated the law. What this group was asking appears to a modern Christian to be a devious ploy, but in their eyes it was a legitimate procedure. In the light of their vow and later events, unless the rabbis found some sort of ablution or release from the vow, one must believe that these people got very hungry.

Acts 23:16-22

There is no information in the narrative as to how Paul's nephew learned about the plot. We know that there were some who were sympathetic to Paul's position on the resurrection, and we know that Joseph of Arimathea had been a member of the Sanhedrin, but he may not have been be alive at this point. Yet someone was a good spy. Neither are we told how the nephew gained entrance to visit Paul. None of this matters, because the issue for the tribune had now become whether he would be able to protect this Roman citizen. The tribune must have realized how critically dangerous the situation might be for the young man, for he ordered him to keep it all quiet. He then proceeded with rather urgent action to move Paul into a safer environment.

[1] Stagg, *The Book of Acts* (Nashville: Broadman Press, 1955), 224.
[2] Rackham, *The Acts of the Apostles* (London: Metheum and Company, Ltd.,1951), 422.
[3] Josephus, *Antiquities of the Jews*, trans. Whitson (Philadelphia: Henry T. Coates and Co), Bk. XV, 11, 5.
[4] Adolph Diessmann, *Light from the Ancient Past*, trans. Strachan (New York and London: Harper and Brothers, 1927), 80ff.
[5] Josephus, *Wars of the Jews*, trans. Whitson (Philadelphia: Henry T. Coates and Co.), Bk. II, XIII, 5.

Chapter 26

Paul Removed from Jerusalem

Acts 23:23-35

The haste with which Claudius Lysias moved to get Paul out of Jerusalem indicates just how dangerous and critical he considered the situation to be. Without even waiting until the next day, he dispatched a large contingent of 470 security guards to move Paul. The combination of cavalry, infantry, and spearmen shows just how seriously Lysias had taken the threat to kill Paul. The terrain was such that an attack should have been made in the hill country, where an ambush would have been easier. The return of part of the guard to Jerusalem when the party reached Antipatris would have made sense, for such a large contingent would no longer be necessary.

As part of the normal procedure, a letter explaining the circumstances that caused him to send a prisoner to a higher authority was drafted. While it was primarily an accurate account, it also stretched the truth a bit to make Lysias look better. The essence of the letter was correct, however, and it formed the basis for a later hearing when the Jewish leaders came down to press their charges.

Acts 24:1-9

Tertullus was a good lawyer, a smooth talker, and an expert in flattery. His entire introduction was designed to get the most favorable hearing possible. There is nothing new in it, and no charges were presented any more forcefully than they had previously been, but the manner in which they were presented was very smooth.

Acts 24:10-21

The opportunity to make his defense before Felix was an occasion in which Paul could bring into focus the main issues of the debate. He did not include that the uproar always occurred when he mentioned his belief that he was responsible for the Gentiles because Tertullus did not mention the issue. The simple statement that he had not defiled the Jewish temple (verse 13) was his only effort to defuse the charge. Therefore, the only issues that he gave credence to were belonging to the Way and belief in the resurrection.

Acts 24:22-24

There is always much that is subjective in the reporting of any event, including biblical literature. Luke indicated that Felix was rather well-informed about the Way. Did this mean that Felix was well-disposed to the movement? Had he dealt with it in a different situation or circumstance? Did he understand the inclusive-exclusive conflict that the new movement generated? None of those questions can be answered, but there is reason to believe that Felix was not overwhelmed by Tertullus' introduction and that he was a bit skeptical about the charges. At any rate, he was concerned that he get the best story he could from the one who had been involved. That he allowed Paul some freedom, and that he felt Paul's friends should have access to him, showed that he did not consider Paul to be any kind of threat. It also implied that he was not at all convinced that the charges were adequate to convict, and that he may have been disposed to believe that he had not been given the entire scenario by the Jews. Some of this may have been because of the letter that Lysias had sent to accompany Paul.

Acts 24:24-27

There are many implications in this last passage, which is primarily meant to convey the change of procurators from Felix to Festus. Who can know all of the anxieties Felix may have had? The very indication that he was "frightened," or perhaps concerned or convicted by the information that Paul had given him regarding "justice, self-control, and judgment," may say much about his own spiritual condition. We would also like to know why Luke concluded that Felix hoped for a bribe. It may have also been the case that since Felix's wife, Druscilla, was a Jewess, she may have helped to inform him about the Way. Druscilla was the daughter of Herod Agrippa I and had previously been married to a Syrian, Azizus, but left him for Felix, who reportedly pursued her for her great beauty.[1] Felix must have been aware that his procuratorship was drawing to a close, so he played the waiting game. When Festus arrived, about 59 C.E., Felix turned the dilemma over to him. However that may be, the narrative is in the midst of showing another great mountain that the movement faced, and how it did not get any negative response and continued to overcome barriers.

Acts 25:1-12

When Claudius Festus came on the scene, he was immediately presented with the dilemma. He, too, had a legal responsibility to protect a Roman citizen and at the same time to attempt to assuage Jewish anger and get off on the right foot with those he was assigned to rule. But before he had time to "get his feet wet," the plot against Paul was renewed. Surely the one who was anxious to get started well with his procuratorship would grant those natives a simple request to transfer Paul's case to Jerusalem. But Festus was much too shrewd a politician to act in haste. So he set up a proper legal hearing to be held in Caesarea, with all parties presenting their cases. Luke was aware that the vow to kill Paul had not been rescinded, and therefore both he and Paul saw through this charade.

It is plain that Paul had seen clearly that he would never get a fair hearing as long as he was in the Jerusalem area. Since the Jews saw their opportunity to persuade the new procurator to grant their petition, they requested that the trial be moved to Jerusalem. Paul must have sensed that Festus was either not fully aware of the situation or that he would not protect him. So when the option for him to be taken to Jerusalem was presented, he immediately rejected it. It would appear that he said something like, "I am currently standing in the Roman Justice Halls, and here the judgment should be made." Initially, he may not have been appealing to the emperor. Whether it was Paul's or Festus' idea that he be sent to Rome, it did relieve Festus of that dilemma. The appeal was not an effort to challenge Festus' decision, which had not yet been made, but an appeal to change the venue, which was the right of a Roman citizen. The details of that right are obscure, but Paul must have had the option. It was his only viable choice at the time and, apparently, Festus was either bound by it or found it to be an excellent way out of the dilemma.

Acts 25:13-27

The hearing before Agrippa II and Bernice was probably just a piece of political etiquette, but it was coupled with the need to write something to send with Paul to Rome. The audience really added nothing to what would later accompany Paul to Rome, but it did provide him an opportunity to proclaim his gospel before a king. Herod and Bernice were brother and sister; they were children of Herod Agrippa I, whose death was recorded in Acts, Chapter 12. Agrippa II was in Rome when his father died in 44 C.E. The Emperor Claudius planned to give him the kingdom but was persuaded not to, and Judea became a province under a procurator. Bernice had been married to her father's brother, another Herod (King of Chalsis), and after he died in 48 B.C. she lived with her brother, apparently in incest. She was later married to Polemon (king of Cilicia) for a short time, but soon returned to her brother. Between 65 and 70 C.E., she attracted the attention of the Roman general Titus and lived with him as his wife. The gossip regarding her lifestyle was apparently rife.[2]

Acts 26:1-32

At the conclusion of the audience, Festus indicated that the entire hearing made no sense to him and that he thought that Paul was mad or insane. Paul had given a brief history of his Jewish background, including both his former life as a persecutor and an account of his conversion. He had tied the message about the suffering servant, the life, death, and resurrection of Jesus, to the prophetic tradition, and then said, "King Agrippa, do you believe the prophets?" Without waiting for an answer, he continued, "I know that you believe." Agrippa responded with a statement like, "Are you trying to make a Christian out of me with a little persuasion?" Nearly all scholars agree that the King James translation of that statement ("Almost thou persuadest me to be a Christian") is not what Agrippa said. Some think that he was saying that Paul was trying to make a Christian out of him in a short time, or with a condensed argument. Paul's response that "whether quickly or not" he could wish that all who heard him could come to the same conclusion he had would indicate that the proper translation is something like that stated above. It also needs to be noted that in the original there would have been no punctuation to indicate either a question or a simple statement, but it probably was a question and not a statement as the KJV interprets it.

The hearing came to the same conclusion that had been seen before. Paul had done nothing to deserve death or even imprisonment. Since his opinion had been elicited, Agrippa decided that if he had not appealed to Caesar, Paul could have been set free. (Apparently, once the appeal had been made it could not be revoked.) At any rate, to have set Paul free in the very area where people were determined to kill him would have produced another tragedy. And Paul's visions — that he would present the good news to royalty — had come true.

[1] *The Harper Study Bible,* footnote 2105.
[2] F.F. Bruce, *The Acts of the Apostles* (Grand Rapids: Wm.B. Eerdmans, 1953), 434.

Chapter 27

Destination Rome

Acts 27:1-12

The narrative concerning the journey to Rome and the shipwreck is certainly one of the most exciting in the book. There were many other times, such as the stoning in Lystra, the beating and imprisonment in Philippi, and the riot in Jerusalem, that must have been filled with anxiety, but this story is a firsthand account of one who was in danger of losing his life to the uncontrollable forces of nature, and it is a vivid expression of that experience.

The journey to Rome was undertaken with Julius in command. The Augustan Cohort appears to have been a special group, somewhat like the modern military police, whose primary duty seems to have been the safety of prisoners. One of the regulations under which they conducted their task was that prisoners were not allowed to escape, on pain of the guards being executed. (One can remember how Herod had the guards executed because Peter had escaped, or the immediate reaction of the jailer at Philippi when he thought that the prisoners had fled.) The centurion had a group of soldiers whose life and death responsibility was to deliver the prisoners to Rome. Whether the century was complete with 100 men we cannot know, but given Luke's report that the number of people on board was 276, it would certainly allow for 100 of them to have been soldiers. In any case, the centurion was the commander, no matter what ship they were on.

Travel by ship was unpredictable. First, there was little power except the wind, which was always uncertain. Luke's account suggests that at first they made good speed and were able to get to the port of Sidon, just up the coast from Caesarea, without difficulty. It is obvious that Julius saw Paul in a much different light than other prisoners, because he granted him certain liberties and apparently had no fear that he would attempt to escape. When they left the coast, the winds blew so that they were forced to make the journey past Cyprus to the port of Myra.

When they finally reached Myra, they changed to a much larger ship, probably a grain ship bound for Italy. The intention was to sail a course westward, as straight as possible, to an Italian port.

But things did not go according to plan. They made it, with great difficulty, to Cnidus, then were blown off course toward the island of Crete. They were rapidly reaching the time of year when all sailing was stopped for the winter because it was unsafe to continue. It is difficult for a twenty-first-century citizen to appreciate the perils they faced. There were no compasses or other instruments to guide them, just the stars. There was no power except that of the wind, for rowing would have been useless, and on a merchant ship there was probably no provision for slaves to row the ship. A military craft might have had slave rowers, but not a merchant ship. Ships were fragile, made of wood, and much more likely to come apart than one might think

So when the wind was against them, they were forced off course nearly 100 miles. They finally sailed under the lee of Crete (to the south of the island), but only with tremendous difficulty. Luke stated that the time of the year was after the fast, which must have been the Jewish Day of Atonement. That date would have come in late September or early October. Sailing was considered unsafe after the middle of September. With great difficulty and uncertainty, they were able to make it to the port of Fair Havens, which was not much of a port at all. It did provide some protection from the wind and was close to the city of Lasaea. Luke was not privy to all of the debate as to where the ship should spend the winter, but he did point out that Paul had at least been in on the discussion and that he had warned against leaving Fair Havens. The ultimate decision was made by the centurion, but he must have talked with those who were more experienced in naval matters. What would be more logical, for the centurion to listen to the captain (pilot) and owner of the ship, or to the prisoner, Paul? So the decision was probably made by the captain, the ship owner, and the centurion. Paul may have had a little input, but it is highly unlikely that a prisoner, even though he had been to sea several times, could have much influence The decision was made to attempt to edge down the coast so that they might winter in a much more desirable port, Phoenix, which would provide protection from both the northwest and the southwest and would be much more appealing to the sailors.

Acts 27:13-20

Luke reported that a moderate or "gentle south wind" came up, and the option immediately was to try to hug the coast around the Caper of Malata, into the Sea of Mesara, and hopefully on to Phoenix, a distance of approximately fifty miles. The gentle south wind may have seemed to present a great opportunity, but scarcely had they cleared the point of Malata than a violent storm fell upon them.

Again, some description of the conditions they found themselves in is necessary. First of all, there was absolutely no possibility of any help. There was no way to know either the speed with which they were moving or the precise direction in which the ship was heading. Anyone who has been in a storm at sea would know that waves of sixty feet or more would pound the little ship mercilessly. Whenever the ship, either bow or stern, would come out of the water, it would smash back down and shudder and groan as if it were coming apart. (This writer has been in two storms on the ocean. One was in the North Atlantic on a Kaiser liberty ship, which seemed to have been welded about every twenty feet. The ship creaked and squealed with every twisting wrench. The other was in the Pacific on a converted oil tanker. The rumor was that the ship would capsize if it rolled more than forty-five degrees, and sometimes it did list close to that mark. Whether there was any truth to the rumor or not, it did create near-panic among troops returning from occupying Japan.) It is not possible to exaggerate the fear that the storm must have produced for Luke, Paul, and others over a period that must have lasted for nearly half a month. No wonder there was no hope. There seems to have been only one small dory, or lifeboat, that could have held only a minute portion of the passengers and crew. Regardless of the faith some of them may have had, those fearful conditions would have produced absolute despair.

Luke named the storm Euraquilo. Its violent winds evidently blew the ship from the northeast toward the southwest. Because these little ships were at the mercy of the storm, it is understandable that the crew had been forced to abandon its goal of reaching Phoenix and simply was trying to make the best of whatever happened to them. It must be remembered that there were no instruments to help when the sky was completely overcast, so they lost all sense of where they were. They knew generally the direction they had been going and that there was a treacherous sand bar, called Syrtis, that stretched for miles into the Mediterranean Sea from the coast of North Africa. At their last sight of land — the little island, Cauda — it looked as though they were being driven in that direction, which would mean that the ship would run aground miles off the coast and be broken apart, so the possibility of surviving was extremely dim. So they did the best they could. They undergirded the ship, which consisted of taking large ropes and slipping them over the bow, then working them back as far as possible and securing them. The process was very uncertain, but the thought was that the ropes could hold at least part of the ship's planks together a little longer. They also began to throw the cargo (probably wheat) overboard to lighten the ship so that it would not run aground as soon and would move more toward the beach. It is also said that soon they threw some of the ship's tackle overboard, for the same reason. Keep in mind that they had no idea where they were, nor could they calculate the speed with which they were being driven. In his typical style, Luke wrote that they were in "no small tempest," and hope for the ship was disappearing.

Acts 27:21-38

It is human to say, "I told you so." After several days, Paul tried to encourage them by saying that he believed that they would lose the ship, but no lives would perish. It was a prophetic proclamation, and to his credit, Paul shared it with the others. After fourteen days of being driven off course (Luke would later write that it was across the Sea of Adria), they must have heard the surf pounding, which made the sailors suspect that they were near land. It was apparently night and, of course, they could have been approaching Syrtis. But they took soundings and discovered that the depth was about 120 feet. When they took soundings again later, the depth had diminished to 90 feet. The logical assumption was that they were approaching land, so four anchors were dropped. The sailors had given up hope that the ship could be saved and plotted to save themselves by escaping in the little boat, but their plan was discovered, perhaps by Paul, who indicated that the remaining passengers needed the expertise of the sailors if they were to save anyone. The soldiers cut the line to the little boat. Little or nothing had been eaten during those taxing days, and knowing that they needed to keep their strength up, Paul urged them to eat.

Acts 27:39-44

When daylight came, they could see land but still had no idea where they were. They planned to beach the ship and, if they could, save themselves. But when they tried to do so, they ran aground at a point of land where opposing currents, beating from opposite directions, were demolishing the ship. The soldiers, aware of their responsibility to deliver the prisoners and trying to make certain that none of them escaped, planned to kill the prisoners. Whether that would have included Paul we cannot know, but the centurion, believing that they could be saved and perhaps wishing to save Paul, rejected the plan and ordered everyone to get ashore any way they could. Some did so by swimming; others used pieces of salvage material and floated ashore. All of them survived.

One remarkable thing about this episode was that the ship had been driven about 600 miles from the time they last saw land (Cauda) until they found themselves at Malta. Not one time had they been able to do any more than guess where they were, and when the ship wrecked, they still did not know what island they were on. The break-up occurred as the ship ran aground on a piece of land that jutted out into the sea, and the currents tore the ship apart. If our calculations are correct, the time frame should place them in early November, and it would have been extremely cold.

Acts 28:1-10

Some commentators have noticed that in the modern age there are no poisonous vipers on Malta. That does not mean that they have never been there. Two things are obvious: first, the natives assumed that the viper was poisonous, and therefore they must have been familiar with certain poisonous species. Second, there is no statement that the viper actually bit Paul. Paul would not have hesitated to shake the thing off his hand. The story does not require any miraculous intervention, but it may have been one of the events that led to the spurious ending of Mark's gospel, which suggests that believers could pick up serpents or even drink poison with immunity. The observation of the natives reflects a superstitious concept that "Justice" as a deity would bring about what should happen, even if this "murderer" had escaped the sea. Of course, they changed their minds when nothing happened to Paul. They were in awe of him and considered him a god.

Acts 28:11-16

Another ship from Alexandria, which had wisely wintered in Malta, became their transportation to the mainland. The ship was named Castor and Pollux, astrological twins that were seen as protectors of sailors. Just what could be expected in terms of the reception in Italy could not be known. The anticipation of Paul's arrival in Rome could certainly have produced some anxiety, both for Paul and for the Christians there. As everyone is aware, Paul had sent the letter we know as The Epistle to the Romans at some earlier point. What kind of reception the letter had gotten was unknown, most likely even to Paul. Neither do we know anything about the Christian community at Puteoli, which was approximately 150 miles from Rome and served as the city's main seaport. However, there were Christians there, and they welcomed Paul. Somehow, the news that Paul was coming had made it to Italy, but considering the difficulty of travel and the delay caused by the shipwreck, messengers could easily have come overland from Jerusalem before Paul arrived. Most of the churches in the first century were "house churches," and there may have been several in Rome. It must have been an encouraging time for Paul when fellow believers from Rome met him at the Market of Appius and Three Taverns.

Surely, Julius delivered Paul to the authorities at once. This would have been a critical time for Paul, not so much for his own safety, but for his hopes of pressing on with the gospel (into Spain?). There may be evidence that Paul was somewhat depressed because he was uncertain about further missionary work. He certainly had much to be grateful for when at least two bodies of believers came from Rome to meet him. We only have the final decision about Paul's quarters, and though he had a personal guard, he was not confined to a prison.

Acts 28:17-32

As he had done whenever possible, Paul began his work in Rome by meeting with the Jews. He could not go to the synagogue, but they could come to him. He laid out his case simply, apparently omitting the information about the conspiracy of the Jews to kill him. According to Luke's account, Paul stated that the Jews objected to him, and therefore he appealed to Nero, who was emperor at this time. Nearly all historians agree that the cruelties of Nero's administration had yet to begin, so there was no reason to think that Paul could not get a fair trial. Apparently, no effort had been made by the Sanhedrin to send any information against Paul to the Jewish community in Rome. Whether they understood that any religious charge would not be considered in a Roman court or simply that they had gotten Paul out of their immediate area is of no importance to the story. The group he called together was composed of leaders of the Jewish community and not just members of the Jewish/Christian community. It is intriguing that they knew that the sect (as they called it) had a bad reputation.

It will be remembered that about a decade earlier, there had been a disturbance among the Jews in Rome over one called "Chrestos," and that Claudius Caesar had decided to banish all Jews from the city. That ban must not have lasted long, nor was it successful, for there is no information that the ban was in effect at this time. So the decision to let Paul explain his position before the Jews set the stage for the completion of Luke's purpose.

Acts 28:23-31

This is the final speech from Paul that Luke gives us. It had about the same effect that many others had. The quotation from Isaiah is about the same as the Synoptic writers used to introduce the need for parables, except that there is no sense in which the blindness and deafness was seen as an act of God. (In this case, it was a decision by the people and dealt not with physical blindness but spiritual.) Again, there is no hint of any disturbance, perhaps because the Roman Jews remembered the previous action of Claudius. This is the sum of what we know about the last part of Paul's ministry. There are those who suggest that he was released and rearrested later, but this theory is fueled by questions about the authorship of some late epistles which some credit to Paul. From what is said here, we may assume that Luke may have planned a third volume, which either was never produced or was not saved. However, the ending of the work is probably the result of what we have described as the purpose of the book. When the gospel story, as Paul taught it, reached the capital city of the then known world, unfettered and unhindered, there was no need for more. Many mountains had been removed, and others had been eroded. It was a simple story that indicated that with faith, no mountain could be such a barrier that it could not be overcome.

There is little reason to believe that the traditional stories of the deaths of both Peter and Paul are suspect. We can certainly believe the tradition that their deaths occurred around 64/65 C.E., during the early part of the persecutions fostered by Nero.

This work has attempted to show that many of those first-century mountains had been overcome. Luke's premise appears to be correct — that the gospel message overcomes all obstacles and moves on unhinderedly.

Bibliography

Allen, John A., *The Epistles of Paul to the Galatians* (London: SCM Press, 1957).

Arndt, William F. and Gingrich, Wilbur, *A Greek-English Lexicon of the New Testament* Chicago: University of Chicago Press, 1955).

Barclay, William, *The Letters to the Corinthians* (Philadelphia: Westminster Press, 1976).

Barclay, William, *The Letters to the Galatians and Ephesians*, Revised Edition (Philadelphia: Westminster Press, 1976).

Barrett C. K., *The First Epistle to the Corinthians* (New York: Harper and Row, 1968).

Beck, Dwight Marion, *Through the Gospels to Jesus* (New York: Harper and Brothers, 1954).

Biddle, Mark, *Missing the Mark: Sin and its Consequences in Biblical Theology* (Nashville: Abingdon Press, 2005).

Bruce F. F., *The Acts of the Apostles* (Grand Rapids: Wm. B Eerdman's, 1953).

Bruce, F.F., *New Century Bible Commentary, I and II Corinthians* (Grand Rapids: Wm. B. Eerdman's, 1980).

Burton, Ernest De Witt, *International Critical Commentary, Galatians* (Edinburgh: T. and T. Clark, 1948.

Charles, R.H., *The Apocrypha and Pseudepigrapha of the Old Testament*, vol. II (London: Oxford Press, 1913).

Deismann, Adolph, *Light from the Ancient Past*, trans. Lionel Strachan (New York and London: Harper and Brothers, 1927).

Foakes-Jackson, F.J., and Lake, Kirsopp, *The Beginnings of Christianity* (London: Macmillan and Co., 1933).

Harper and Collins Study Bible, NRSV (London: Harper and Collins, 1989).

Josephus, Flavius, *The Antiquities of the Jews*, trans. William Whitson (Philadelphia: Henry T. Coates and Co.).

Josephus, Flavius, *The Wars of the Jews*, trans. William Whitson (Philadelphia: Henry T. Coates and Co.).

Lightfoot, J. B., *The Epistle of Paul to the Galatians* (Grand Rapids: Zondervan, 1965).

Macgregor, G.H.C., *The Interpreter's Bible*, vol. ix (New York and Nashville: Abingdon Press, 1954).

Manson, William, *The Epistle to the Hebrews* (London: Hodder and Staughton, 1953).

The Mishnah, trans. Herbert Danby (London: Oxford Press, 1954).

Moffatt, James, *The Epistle of Paul to the Galatians* (New York and London: Harper and Brothers, 1934).

Oesterley, W.O.E., *A History of Israel*, vol. II (Oxford: Clarendon Press, 1951).

Rackham, Richard Belward, *The Acts of the Apostles* (London: Metheun and Company, Ltd., 1951).

Ramsey, W. M., *The Church in the Roman Empire* (London: Hodder and Staughton, 1893).

Robertson, Archibald T., *A Grammar of the Greek New Testament in the Light of Historical Research* (Nashville: Broadman Press, 1934).

Smith, David, *The Life and Letters of St. Paul* (New York: Harper and Brothers, 1950).

Stamm, Raymond, *The Interpreter's Bible*, vol. 10 (New York and Nashville: Abingdon Press, 1953).

Weatherhead, Leslie, *The Will of God* (Nashville: Abingdon Press, 1972).

www.ingramcontent.com/pod-product-compliance
Lightning Source LLC
Chambersburg PA
CBHW070919180426
43192CB00038B/1858